WINNING THE
ENTREPRENEUR
SHUFFLE
Building Blocks for New-preneurs
Textbook Edition

By Dr. Iria L. Abram

EPHRIAM HOUSE, Inc. | Atlanta, GA

ephriamhouse.com

Published by EPHRIAM HOUSE, Atlanta, Georgia.

www.ephriamhouse.com

EPHRIAM HOUSE, and the logo image, are trademarks of Ephriam House, Inc.

Created in the United States of America

Cover Design by Dr. Iria L. Abram

ISBN-13: 978-0692-188-071

ISBN-10: 069218807X

Abram, Iria L. (2018) *Winning the Entrepreneur Shuffle: Building Blocks for New-Preneurs*, Textbook Edition. Atlanta, GA: Ephriam House, Inc.

What the Experts are Saying

"It is my recommendation that anyone who is in business read this book! I've been in business for over twenty years and Winning the Entrepreneur Shuffle: Building Blocks for New-preneurs has been a refresher of foundational tools that have and will allow any business to thrive. If you're looking to birth your vision, or reboot an old one, Winning the Entrepreneur Shuffle is the guide for you!

Alycia J. Moorman, BA, MS
Owner|CEO of Salon Rejuvenate
coifrejuvenator.com

"Winning the Entrepreneur Shuffle...WOW! What an amazing journey Dr. Abram takes us on in the building blocks to being a successful entrepreneur. You will be challenged in your creativity, highly stimulated to be more than ordinary, but most of all motivated to move forward. If you're tired of the nine-to-five, punching a time clock, unhappy workplace, or if you've had a burning idea or two that you know would do well, this resource tool kit will be your guide to becoming your own boss!"

Angelita P. Howard, MS, MA, EdD
Independent Education Consultant
angelitahoward.com

"In this book you will find a road map to develop, grow, expand, and see heights beyond the imagination. In the end Dr. Abram has creatively helped you to find your way to your dream."

Glenise Harris-Wilson, BS, MA, EdD
Pathway Int'l Institute of Pastoral Counseling & Life Coaching
linkedin.com/in/gleniseharriswilsonaccelerate

"In her book, author Dr. Iria Abram, has taken on the task of not only laying the foundation for people of Christian Faith that desire to become Entrepreneurs, but also providing the necessary building blocks to become a B.U.S.I.N.E.S.S.P.E.R.S.O.N. James 2:26 tells us that faith without works is dead. It is one thing to have a dream; but it takes WORK to fulfill your vision. Through this incredible read, Dr. Iria Abram will provide the necessary tools that will allow you to find your niche' so that you can be included in the 5% of the general population who are actually living their dreams."

Chris Bowen, BA, MA, DMin

Author | Coach | Mentor
drchrisbowen.com

"Iria Abram's entrepreneurial text is a venerable repository of information for thinking about, launching and growing your personal business. Entrepreneurs need all the help they can get to maintain and grow their business. So much is at stake. Dr. Abram captures the essential building blocks for entrepreneurs and orders them in a way that is practical, pragmatic and principled. As a colleague, she has consistently proven to be a thought leader and a person of efficacious inquiry. The brightness of her reflection produces an incredible forward moving momentum. Whatever she writes will help you! Whatever she writes from her own experiences will bless you immeasurably."

Brian Keith Hodges, BA, MA, DEdMin

Chair | Dept. of Religious Studies, Beulah Heights University
Senior Pastor | Gathering of Champions Church

"Winning the Entrepreneur Shuffle by Dr. Iria L. Abram will teach you how to shuffle the five factors of production: (1) natural resources, (2) labor, (3) physical capital, (4) human capital, and (5) entrepreneurship into building blocks that can equip you to join the "New-preneurs" of the 21st Century. Dr. Abram's experience and insights will open a new understanding of how to gain and sustain the competitive advantage in your entrepreneurial endeavors."

Rodney B. Jackson, BA, MDiv, PsyD

Founder|CEO of Transformation & Empowerment Coaching
Linkedin.com/in/dr-rodney-b-jackson-185b22114

Acknowledgments

With heartfelt appreciation, this book is dedicated first, back to God who is my life's CEO and "SO" much more, to my amazing husband, Vincent Augusta Abram, and to our brilliant sons, Isaac Michael Abram and Elisha Ephriam Abram. Also to our incredible parents who support us in every way: in special memory of my dear mom, Mother Maggie Lee Estell (12/12/1952 – 8/3/2016); my loving father Evangelist Iria Ephriam, Jr.; and to Mr. and Mrs. James Michael and Delores Spaulding. It takes a village, and our village rocks!

Special Acknowledgements:

Cornelia Sharon Estell

Marceise Gabriel Moore

Pastor & Mrs. Earl William & Nancy Estell

Capri Cypress Estell

Earl William Estell, Jr.

Ira Earl Campbell

Joshua Earl Campbell

Ira Earl Campbell, Jr.

Iria Lawuance Ephriam

Jamie Michelle Spaulding

Lee Michael Spaulding

Elder Oleria Anne Treadwell

Rev. Dr. Percy D. Johnson, Jr.

Contents

WINNING THE
ENTREPRENEUR
SHUFFLE

PREFACE:

Building Blocks to

Becoming a

B.U.S.I.N.E.S.S.P.E.R.S.O.N.

More than ever before, entrepreneurship is growing increasingly popular. More people are convinced that their path to living a fulfilling life is not confined to traditional employment. For all *New-preneurs* and anyone else who has been contemplating whether or not to step into the startup space, this is the perfect time to get in the race and win! For the faith community, there are often teachings on having "vision" and "dreams" for the future, but that does not always equate to individuals being equipped with tools and knowledge of what to do with those visions and dreams to see them actually proliferate and come into being. Notably, some organizations, churches and ministries are doing a stellar job at educating their members and communities on business matters. However, for others…not so much. One of the functions of this book is to be a bridge between the Christian faith community and the general startup ecosystem. By using the information in this book to lay a foundation, and by setting each of the provided building blocks in their proper place, one will have the best chance of winning at their entrepreneurial goals and desired outcomes.

All signs are pointing toward success for new entrepreneurs. According to Forbes (a global media company focusing on business, investing, technology, entrepreneurship, leadership and lifestyle), here are a few reasons why: (1)

venture capital investments are the highest they've ever been; (2) amendments to intellectual property laws are leaning in the favor of small businesses; (3) explosive growth in the Artificial Intelligence (AI) market is expected to create a multi-billion dollar industry, providing plenty of opportunities for new businesses; (4) the rise in freelancers and on-demand project management (Fiverr, UpWork, Freelancer, etc.) are affording entrepreneurs the ability to produce goods and services that can compete against big business and their intimidating marketing budgets; (5) big business is showing support for startups with initiatives like transparency in their pricing and licensing terms; and (6) Intellectual Property (IP) accounts for almost 40% of the US Gross Domestic Product (GDP), and for over 30% of the total national employment![i] This means that any person with a great idea, a vision, a dream, or a passion has a fair chance to achieve success! And not just the success of materializing a goal—as rewarding as that may be—but wealth creation is possible (cue the fireworks!) It is at this point, early on in the business development process, that you need to legally register your business with the secretary of state. Note: This business registration must be renewed annually. You can do this as well as register a business name, or secure an Employee Identification Number (EIN), all online. A quick web search will take you to the appropriate web site according to your state of residence.

As exciting as starting a new business may be, there is a serious need to stop and evaluate all of your life's circumstances, both great potential and realistic limitations. This pursuit, if not managed properly, can lead to being completely out of balance. Necessary financial investment, time demands and the need to learn entirely new sectors of business can seem overwhelming. However, the successful entrepreneur must find sensible and creative ways to maintain peace and balance while keeping perspective of their goals, the tasks at hand and their ultimate vision. The best way to safeguard sanity and overall wellbeing are through various practices of "self-care!" Self-care can manifest in any number of expressions. The following are examples of self-care habits that may help reduce stress and organize responsibilities:

- Prayer and meditation
- Turning the phone off at night
- Exercise and healthy dieting
- Being intentional about scheduling time for your favorite hobby, sport, or activity
- Taking sabbaticals and vacations
- Identifying your support system

Each person is different, and everyone will have a different scenario that they must balance. However, they all must include some measure of self-care to endure and sustain the journey of entrepreneurship and the world of business.

Doing business looks different today than it did a decade ago. The phenomenon of social media, digital marketing and automation have leveled the playing field. Any person or business willing to be persistent and resilient can do great things. With that said, there are certain tenants of business that are universal and just cannot be ignored. Here, these things are considered to be *Building Blocks*. In this book, fourteen building blocks to help a new-preneur to become a B.U.S.I.N.E.S.S.P.E.R.S.O.N will be explored by Dr. Iria L. Abram, founder and CEO of EPHRIAM HOUSE; a business consulting company that has provided professional services for over thirteen years. Since before *Photoshop*, *Facebook* and *iPhone* became household phrases, EPHRIAM HOUSE has been helping individuals to bring structure to their dreams and formulate plans to build businesses and generate revenue. Certain aspects of the process have proven to be unchanging and necessary steps for a businessperson to think through. This book opens up each of these steps, or building blocks, on an introductory level to provide the best possible start for anyone who wants to turn their entrepreneurial vision and dream into reality.

---

[i] David Pridham, (January 10, 2018), Entrepreneurs: Here's Good News For 2018. *Forbes.com*. Retrieved from https://www.forbes.com/sites/davidpridham/2018/01/10/entrepreneurs-heres-good-news-for-2018/#3ead46d76659

BLOCK 1

B.U.S.I.N.E.S.S.P.E.R.S.O.N.

Build a Foundation

The initial matter to address is clarifying exactly what the endeavor into entrepreneurship really is. There are fundamental differences between entrepreneurship and small business ownership that business owners need to understand. Every reader should be asking, *"What exactly am I getting myself into?"* In short, an entrepreneur is someone who exercises the initiative to organize a venture to benefit from, and as the decision maker, decides what, how and how much of a good or service will be produced.[ii] In addition, an entrepreneur supplies risk capital as a risk taker and monitors and controls the business activities. The entrepreneur is usually a sole proprietor, a partner, or the one who owns the majority of shares in an incorporated venture. This differs from a traditional small business because an entrepreneur usually assumes full risk and financial responsibility, where a small business may have a lender or venture capitalist (VC) assuming the financial risk through startup funding.

According to economist Joseph Alois Schumpeter (1883-1950), entrepreneurs are not necessarily motivated by profit but regard it as a standard for measuring achievement or success. An entrepreneur has other key performance indicators (KPIs) that they are focused on attaining. This concept aligns with faith based initiatives. It's all about fulfilling the mission. For the faith community, entrepreneurship is *Christian*

Vocation. The word *vocation* comes from the Latin word "vocare," which means "to call." It is a strong feeling of suitability for a particular career or occupation, especially one regarded as worthy and requiring dedication.[iii]

So what is *Christian vocation?* As a believer following God's model, being in a Christian vocation means being able to reveal God to the world through one's work. It is an endeavor built on Godly principles such as faith, gifts, talents, anointing and purpose where the ultimate goal is connected to a Christian mandate such as fulfilling the great commission, or sharing the gospel message. It is important to note that the Godly model, such as the creation narrative for example, reflects that God not only worked, but that God worked well, took pleasure in the work, evaluated it and then rested! #balance!

In building a foundation, it is important to know why your new venture is being formed. Having an established vision and mission can become a life-line for an entrepreneur in difficult times when defining decisions must be made. A clear vision and mission statement help a business or individual to know who they are and what they are doing so that they do not find themselves off course and lost in the shuffle. A vision statement should describe the future state of the business or organization. It should point less to where the company is presently, and more toward where it aspires to be. A mission statement can include a brief description of what the business exists to accomplish and how that is going to happen. It may not be until after reading block three that a vision and mission statement can be established.

[ii] "Entrepreneur," BusinessDirectory.com, retrieved from: http://www.businessdictionary.com/definition/entrepreneur.html

[iii] "Vocare," OxfordDictionaries.com, retrieved from: https://en.oxforddictionaries.com/definition/vocation

Empowering Scripture

"Anyone who listens to my teaching and follows it is wise, like a person who builds a house on solid rock. Though the rain comes in torrents and the floodwaters rise and the winds beat against that house, it won't collapse because it is built on bedrock. But anyone who hears my teaching and doesn't obey it is foolish, like a person who builds a house on sand. When the rains and floods come and the winds beat against that house, it will collapse with a mighty crash."

Matthew 7:24-27

Write now! Don't forget the ideas you have while reading this section:_____

_____

_____

_____

_____

_____

_____

_____

_____

_____

_____

_____

_____

_____

_____

_____

_____

_____

_____

_____

BLOCK 2

B.**U**.S.I.N.E.S.S.P.E.R.S.O.N.

Understand the Problem

BLOCK 2: Understand the Problem

A business provides a product or service that solves a problem. There will always be someone tasked with finding a better, faster, more cost efficient, more engaging, more relevant, or smarter way to do something. Therefore, in building a new business, the entrepreneur must be able to articulate what problem it is that they can help someone to solve. A business concept is great when it is the answer to somebody's prayer! Therefore, the entrepreneur is in the solutions business and there are several ways to determine which direction to take in deciding where they have the opportunity to make an impact and generate revenue. However, the most effective way is to find a *niche*.

A niche is a smaller section of the larger global market created through a process of narrowing data called *data segmentation*. Chapter seven reviews this in more detail. Knowing one's niche can help them resist the Messiah Complex—trying to save the whole world—and help them to more quickly identify the concerns they really want to address. A niche is the focus of the products and services a business provides. Examples are:

- Dog owners

- Sports Enthusiasts

- Senior citizens

- Persons within a certain income margin

- Military veterans

- Religious affiliations

- Business owners

- Home owners

- Person's living in a certain location

- Couples with no children

Furthermore, a niche can also be introspective and refer to a specific or unique skill or talent the business owner is equipped to offer. For example:

- Woodworking handmade birdhouses

- Magician hosting magic shows

- Thesis editing and paper formatting

There is no limit to the specifications that can be considered in finding a niche. Russel Brunson, founder of *Clickfunnels.com*, teaches about a concept he describes as "red and blue water." He says that red water in marketing is likened to bloody water dense with tons of shark all fighting each other and ripping each other to shreds trying to capture the same prey. Blue water then is the open ocean far out and away from all other hunters where a single shark may find its prey in peace. Finding a niche is like finding that peaceful blue water.

With a defined niche, the next step is to provide a solution to a problem in which that audience is facing. So if a business focuses on dog owners, there is a vast array of things that need a solution.

- Veterinarian care
- Food
- Exercise and safe play areas
- Dog houses
- Training
- Dog walkers and sitters
- Clothing
- Toys

This is how a market is narrowed down. The entrepreneur knows they want to start a business that serves dog owners, and may decide to focus on selling dog houses. This may seem narrow enough, but there are more decisions to be made!

- Will they actually design and build custom dog houses?

- Will they have a B&M (brick and mortar) physical location, or an online store, or both?
- Will they stock pile dog houses in a warehouse or only sell items that the manufacturer can ship directly to the customer?
- Will they provide repair services for persons with damaged dog houses?

The clearer an entrepreneur is on who they are and what problem they are prepared to solve, the better their chances of success.

Empowering Scripture

"Therefore thus says the Lord GOD, "Behold, I am laying in Zion a stone, a tested stone, A costly cornerstone for the foundation, firmly placed. He who believes in it will not be disturbed."

Isaiah 28:16

Write now! Don't forget the ideas you have while reading this section:_____

_____

_____

_____

_____

_____

_____

_____

_____

_____

_____

_____

_____

_____

_____

_____

_____

_____

_____

BLOCK 3

B.U.**S̲**.I.N.E.S.S.P.E.R.S.O.N.

S̲tart Dreaming

BLOCK 3: Start Dreaming

Once an entrepreneur identifies the problem they want to find a solution to, then they must engage the process of brainstorming and product innovation. This is where the solution to the problem is crafted through the process of *ideation*. Ideation is the brainwork of considering the possibilities. Dreaming and envisioning the solution in action helps to kick-start creative ideas. It is imagining the customer wearing the item, or using the software. In *Lean Ideation* author Paul J. Rowean teaches that the most important part of this process is considering the voice of the customer (VOC).[iv] The dreaming and contemplation of what the solution looks like must be informed by what the customer has communicated that they need. To responsibly collect this invaluable information from customers, or potential customers, the businessperson can issue surveys to their current clientele, or data-mine consumer reports for information reflecting the customer experience with products or services that are similar to what is being considered. Reports on consumer trends are available to the public by subscription to sites like *ConsumerReports.com*. There are several free sources available.

The inception of some endeavors begin with a single person while others are birthed from groups of key people all lending their collective passion, experience and drive toward problem solving. Either way there are several methods of ideation and ways of dreaming that can be employed in this process. The following are thirty methods of brainstorming that can be helpful.

1. **Prayer and Meditation.** Focus on solving the problem, and be prepared to note what comes to mind and what God is saying. Try to visualize it.

2. **Group Ideation**. The most common method is a group brainstorming session. Parameters may or may not be required. Multiple brains can be better than one.

3. **Medici Effect.** Put goals alongside similar goals from different contexts and identify like challenges. For example: if considering how to open a law firm, look at people who opened medical practices, or consulting firms. The point is to look for any universal commonalities that can be applied.

4. **Resources Unlimited.** What could be done if time, money, employees and travel were all limitless resources for the business?

5. **Challenger.** Write down every assumption about the business venture and challenge each one of them. For example: a team is considering opening an ice cream parlor. They would ask, Why ice cream? Does it have to be desert? Why a parlor? Can we have it delivered by a third party? Why now? Etc.

6. **Exaggeration**. How would a goal be reached if it is ten times, or a thousand times larger? What if it is a tenth, or a

thousandth its current size? For example: a property management company needs fifty renters to occupy a condominium community. What would they do differently if they needed five hundred renters? Or only five?

7. **Escape Thinking.** This is a variation of Challenger method. Look at the assumptions behind the goal you are trying to achieve, then flip that assumption around and look at your goal from that new angle. For example: you want to earn more income from selling books. Your assumption may be 'People buy books for themselves'. Flip the assumption around such that 'People do NOT buy books for reading'. What will this lead to? You may end up with people buy books as gifts, for collection purposes, etc. Another assumption may be 'People read books'. The flip side of this assumption may be people look at books (drawings). Escaping from these assumptions will bring you to a different realm of thought on how to achieve your goal.

8. **Mind Mapping.**[v] Mind mapping is a visual tool for enhancing the brainstorming process. In essence, you're drawing a picture of the relationships among and between ideas. It's easy to find mind mapping software online. The reality, though, is that a large piece of paper and a few markers can also do the job.

9. **Reverse Brainstorming.** Ordinary brainstorming asks participants to solve problems. Reverse brainstorming asks

participants to come up with great ways to cause a problem. Start with the problem and ask "how could we cause this?" Once you have a list of great ways to create problems, you're ready to start solving them! Learn about how to run a reverse brainstorming session.

10. **Gap Filling**. Start with a statement of where you are. Then write a statement of where you'd like to be. How can you fill in the gap to get to your goal? Your participants will respond with a wide range of answers from the general to the particular. Collect them all, and then organize them to develop a vision for action.

11. **Drivers Analysis**. Work with your group to discover the drivers behind the problem you're addressing. What's driving client loyalty down? What's driving the competition? What's driving a trend toward lower productivity? As you uncover the drivers, you begin to catch a glimpse of possible solutions.

12. **SWOT Analysis**. SWOT Analysis identifies organizational strengths, weaknesses, opportunities and threats. Usually, it's used to decide whether a potential project or venture is worth undertaking. In brainstorming, it's used to stimulate collaborative analysis. What are our real strengths? Do we have weaknesses that we rarely discuss? New ideas can come out of this tried-and-true technique.

13. **The Five Whys**. Another tool that's often used outside of brainstorming, the Five Whys can also be effective for getting thought processes moving forward. Simply start with a problem you're addressing and ask "why is this happening?" Once you have some answers, ask "why does this happen?" Continue the process five times (or more), digging deeper each time until you've come to the root of the issue. Dig into the details of this process.

14. **Starbursting**. Create a six pointed star. At the center of the star, write the challenge or opportunity you're facing. At each point of the star, write one of the following words: who, what, when, where, why and how. Use these words to generate questions. Who are our happiest clients? What do our clients say they want? Use the questions to generate discussion.

15. **Brain-Netting** (Online Brainstorming). Perhaps not surprisingly, brain netting involves brainstorming on the Internet. This requires someone to set up a system whereby individuals can share their ideas privately, but then collaborate publicly. There are software companies that specialize in just such types of systems, like *Slack* or *Google Docs*. Once ideas have been generated, it may be good to come together in person, but it's also possible that online idea generation and discussion will be successful on its own.

This is an especially helpful approach for remote teams to utilize, though any team can make use of it.

16. **Brain-writing** (or Slip Writing). The brain writing process involves having each participant anonymously write down ideas on index cards. The ideas can then be randomly shared with other participants who add to or critique the ideas. Alternatively, the ideas can be collected and sifted by the management team. This approach is also called "Crawford Slip Writing," as the basic concept was invented in the 1920's by a professor named Crawford.

17. **Collaborative Brain-writing**. Write your question or concern on a large piece of paper, and post it in a public place. Ask team members to write or post their ideas when they are able, over the course of a week. Organize the ideas on your own or with your group's involvement after that week.

18. **Role Play Brainstorming**. What would you do if you were someone else? Your parent? Your teacher? Your manager? Your partner? Your best friend? Your enemy? Etc. Ask your participants to imagine themselves in the role of a person whose experience relates to your brainstorming goal (a client, upper management, a service provider). Act out a scene, with participants pretending to take the other's point of view. Why might they be dissatisfied? What would it take for them to feel better about their experience or outcomes?

19. **Reverse Thinking**. This creative approach asks, "What would someone else do in our situation?" Then imagine doing the opposite. Would it work? Why or why not? Does the "usual" approach really work well, or are there better options?

20. **Iconic Figure Storming**. What if you were an iconic figure of the past? Buddha? Jesus? Krishna? Maya Angelou? Albert Einstein? Thomas Edison? Mother Theresa? Princess Diana? Barack Obama? Steve Jobs? Bill Gates? Warren Buffet? George Lopez? Etc. How would you think about your situation? What would that individual do to manage the challenge or opportunity you're discussing? How might that figure's approach work well or poorly?

21. **Step Ladder Brainstorming**. Start by sharing the brainstorming challenge with everyone in the room. Then send everyone out of the room to think about the challenge—except two people. Allow the two people in the room to come up with ideas for a short period of time, and then allow just one more person to enter the room. Ask the new person to share their ideas with the first two before discussing the ideas already generated. After a few minutes ask another person to come in, and then another. In the long run, everyone will be back in the room—and everyone will have had a chance to share his or her ideas with colleagues.

22. **Round Robin Brainstorming**. A "round robin" is a game in which everyone gets a chance to participate. In the case of brainstorming that means everyone (1) must share an idea and (2) wait until everyone else has shared before suggesting a second idea or critiquing ideas. This is a great way to encourage shy (or uninterested) individuals to speak up while keeping dominant personalities from taking over the brainstorming session.

23. **Rapid Ideation**. This simple technique can be surprisingly fruitful. Ask the individuals in your group to write down as many ideas as they can in a given period of time. Then either have them share the ideas aloud or collect responses. Often, you'll find certain ideas popping up over and over again; in some cases these are the obvious ideas, but in some cases they may provide some revelations.

24. **Trigger Storming**. This variant on the round robin approach starts with a "trigger" to help people come up with thoughts and ideas. Possible triggers include open ended sentences or provocative statements. For example: "Client issues always seem to come up when _____," or "The best way to solve client problems is to pass the problem along to someone else."

25. **Charrette**. Imagine a brainstorming session in which thirty-five people from six different departments are all struggling to come up with viable ideas. The process is time

consuming, boring and—all too often—unfruitful. The Charrette method breaks up the problem into smaller chunks, with small groups discussing each element of the problem for a set period of time. Once each group has discussed one issue, their ideas are passed on to the next group who builds on them. By the end of the Charrette, each idea may have been discussed five or six times—and the ideas discussed have been refined.

26. **"What If" Brainstorming**. What if this problem came up 100 years ago? How would it be solved? What if Superman were facing this problem? How would he manage it? What if the problem were fifty times worse—or much less serious than it really is? What would we do? These are all different types of "what if" scenarios that can spur radically creative thinking—or at least get people laughing and working together!

27. **Time Travel**. How would you deal with this if you were in a different time period? 10 years ago? 100 years ago? 1,000 years ago? 10,000 years ago? How about in the future? 10 years later? 100 years later? 1,000 years later? 10,000 years later?

28. **Teleportation**. What if you were facing this problem in a different place? Different country? Different geographic region? Different universe? A different plane of existence? How would you handle it?

29. **Attribute change**. How would you think about this if you were a different gender? Age? Race? Intellect? Height? Weight? Nationality? With each attribute change, you become exposed to a new spectrum of thinking you were subconsciously closed off from.[vi]

30. **Abram Method**. This is the first mention of this approach. Brainstorming according to the Abram method asks how many different ways God can be glorified in the endeavor. Regarding Christian Vocation- How does your company serve the kingdom? Are there any key scriptures or biblical principles? Any church or organizational affiliations? Any goals for local or global missions?

Taking the time to dream exhaustively and think extensively about the business can only help strengthen its formation and development. Revisit any vision or mission notes and see if they align with what you received from your brainstorming.

[iv] Paul J. Rowean, (2016), *Lean Ideation: Successful New Product Development and Commercialization* (Oakbrook Terrace, IL: Green Ivy Publishing), Chapter 2-4.

[v] Lisa Jo Rudy, (September 7, 2016), 19 Top brainstorming Techniques, *Businessttps.tutsplus.com*, retrieved from: https://business.tutsplus.com/articles/top-brainstorming-techniques--cms-27181.

[vi] Celestine Chua, (n.d), 25 Useful brainstorming Techniques, *PersonalExcellence.co,* retrieved from: https://personalexcellence.co/blog/brainstorming-techniques/

Empowering Scripture

"And he has filled him with the Spirit of God, with wisdom, with understanding, with knowledge and with all kinds of skills."

Exodus 35:31

"For with God nothing shall be impossible."

Luke 1:37

Write now! Don't forget the ideas you have while reading this section:_____

_____

_____

_____

_____

_____

_____

_____

_____

_____

_____

_____

_____

_____

_____

_____

_____

_____

_____

_____

_____

BLOCK 4

B.U.S.**I**.N.E.S.S.P.E.R.S.O.N.

Invent Products & Services

BLOCK 4: Invent Products & Services

Hopefully, after identifying a niche and going through one or more of the brainstorming exercises in the last section you generated a list of products and services you'd like to create. These have to align with the target audience, which is reviewed in more detail in block seven. The target audience has to be able to afford the products and services, as well as afford to continue to come back for more! Products and services create the backbone for any business. No matter the size of the business, one of the first things a business person will do is decide what the business will offer. These will be either products, services or a combination of both.

New products and services are the lifeblood of all businesses. Investing in their development isn't optional—it is crucial to business growth and profitability. This is also when the logo, tag lines and branding messages are developed. However, embarking on the development process is risky. It needs considerable planning and organization. There are key stages in the lifecycle of products and services that indicate when the time is right for a business to start the development process. One of the most important ways to sustain profit in a niche-related business is to create new products and services that its target audience will be eager to buy. This can be accomplished in a number of ways.

The most obvious way to begin is with a new product launch. If a niche is understood well, chances are there is a pretty good idea of what that specific market really needs and how much they are willing to pay for it. In other words, the goal is not only to create new products, but products that are certain to sell. There are five key stages in the lifecycle of any product or service:

1. Development. At this point a product or service is only an idea and a company is investing heavily in research and development.
2. Introduction. To actually launch the product or service a company spent heavily to market.
3. Growth. The product or service is establishing itself. There are few competitors, sales are growing and profit margins are good. Now is the time to think on how to reduce the costs of delivering the new product.
4. Maturity. Sales growth is slowing or has even stopped. Production and marketing costs were reduced, but increased competition has driven down prices. Now is likely to be the best time to invest in a new product.
5. Decline. New and improved products or services are on the market and competition is high. Sales fall and profit margins decline. Increased marketing will have little impact on sales and won't be cost-effective unless new markets are identified.

Identifying where products or services are in the five stage lifecycle above is central to profitability. Effective research into markets and competitors will help with this, which leads to good news – the lifecycle of a product or service can be extended by investing in an *extension strategy*! The following are options for extension:

- Increase promotional spending.
- Introduce minor innovations–perhaps by adding extra features or updating the design.
- Seek new markets.

Ultimately this only delays a product or service's decline. Remember, this is only an *extension* strategy. Ideally, there should always be new products or services to introduce as others decline so that there is a better chance of at least one thing showing a sales peak.

There is a lot at stake when developing a new product or service. To minimize risks and allocate investment and resources wisely, consider a number of factors:

- Will the new product or service meet customers' specifications? For example: Consider its design, ease of use and performance benefits.
- How technologically feasible is the product or service? Are the design and manufacturing requirements realistic?
- Is there clarity about what the business hopes to achieve with the new product or service? Does it meet the strategy

outlined in the business plan and play to the business' strengths?

The clearer a company is about plans, the better the risks can be analyzed. The following tips may also be helpful:

- Consult team members about development plans - they may contribute insights that others have overlooked.

- Seek the views of suppliers and other business associates - their specialist expertise could be invaluable.

- Test lots of ideas at the start of a project - it costs relatively little to assess which are most promising, but make sure to stop work on ideas that don't meet certain criteria before committing a lot of time and resources.

- Ask the best customers what they think of the plans.

- Consider the regulatory framework within which the new product or service will operate.

- Don't overlook the environmental impact of the plans. Will it increase or decrease local employment? Will it cause any harmful waste or toxic water run-off? Etc.

- Look beyond a new product or service's immediate potential and consider the longer term.

New products and services have to offer benefits that meet customers' needs. Market research, using techniques such as surveys and focus groups, will help do this. Remember that although the end user of the product or service might be the most important customer, the needs of other parties will also have to be taken into account. For example: If a businessowner was planning a new DIY product, they would need to consider how retailers would stock it as well as how it would benefit professional decorators. If they're creating a toy, they should consider what parents, as well as the children, will think of it.

Not only must the customers' needs be met, it has to be done so in a way that is better than the alternatives offered by the competition. The new product or service needs a unique selling proposition (USP)—a feature or detail that makes it stand out in the marketplace. Before entering the market the following should be determined:

- How customers' needs are currently met and why customers would choose your product or service rather than that of the competition's—both now and in the future.
- What risks you are prepared to take to launch your product or service into this market.

Establishing a pricing strategy for a new product or service is an important part of the development process. At the very moment it is decided to take an idea forward, stop and consider the pricing, as it will determine how much can be afforded to invest in the project. Take the following factors into account:

- The benefits, or value, to the customer compared with what the competition has to offer.
- Will the price be one that customers are prepared to pay?
- Whether or not it is "first to market." Is the

product or service revolutionary or following a market trend?

- Consider the selling channels, which will affect promotional spending and distribution costs.
- The speed with which the product or service needs to be completed and established.
- The expected lifecycle of product or service.
- Whether revenue from this product is covering any other costs.

Developing new products and services is an inherently risky process. Plan any investment carefully and strictly control all costs.

The following is helpful:

- Factor any future investment in products and services into the strategic business plan.
- Plan exactly where this investment will be directed.
- Justify expenditure on every project.
- Manage costs and expenses meticulously.

Before making investment decisions, consider how much the business stands to gain from a compete product or service. Weigh this against the risks you face.

One way to minimize risks is to phase (taking one step at a time) investments in projects. At the end of each phase, review the project to identify the various products or services that are unlikely to be successful before more resources are wasted. This is more useful than most may think: if a product or service fails to meet established criteria, the entire project should be ditched! However, if it does meet the criteria, resources sufficient to enable it to reach the next stage can be allocated. Remember, this is Christian vocation, so the principles of stewardship apply! Note: A range of government grants and tax breaks are available for research on new product development.

In thinking of costs, it is essential to keep a close eye on it when you develop new products and services to avoid expenses spiraling out of control; which can happen without drawing notice until it is way too late. To avoid this, estimate development costs in advance, and be sure to stick to the budget! Monitor expenditures throughout the development process and introduce *phased* investment. There are two main ways to estimate costs: (1) a top-down approach where you consider previous comparable projects and use them as a benchmark; and (2) a bottom-up approach where all team members agree on the costs they expect to incur with one project manager, who will then estimate the total cost.

Remember that costs could include staffing, materials, technology, product design, market research, prototyping and incremental overhead costs. You want to earn enough to replenish these costs, so do not miss or overlook every imaginable revenue opportunity. Therefore, in addition of the physical product or hands-on service, ask if there is a site or blog for the business. If so, consider putting e-books together by topics. *"How to..."* titles are extremely attractive to most audiences. Consider different levels of learners in the same niche, such as beginners, intermediates and advanced users. Look at what the competition is selling, and at what price points. In this case you have two choices: (1) charge less and give the same type of product or service, or (2) charge more due to your expertise in the niche and the quality of what you'll offer.

Furthermore, regarding costs, bundling works for all paid products. Again, there are two choices: (1) you can sell one main product and bundle a range of very attractive bonuses together, such as worksheets, hand-outs, templates, info-graphics and more; or (2) you can group two of your most popular products and services together to create an all new offer that the target market will be eager to buy. Add some fabulous bonuses on top of that and see how much profit can be made from niche-related products and services.

The more income streams running through your business and into the bank account the better. There are possibilities to explore that may open up your business to multiple revenue streams. The following are just a few.

1. Wholesale the product or service: If retail

has been the only option, it is worth a look into wholesaling as well. Wholesaling is selling your product in larger quantities and at a lower price to retailers and distributors for resale in other stores. Your industry and its competitiveness will dictate how hard it is to break into this market. To get started, develop sell sheets, wholesale pricing, and vendor agreements before you approach buyers.

2. Design an affiliate program for your company. An affiliate program is a built-in sales force without the hefty pay rates or personnel issues. All you need to do is sign up using a site like e-Junkie, Clickbank or Share-A-Sale, register your product and dictate your terms. People will sign up to sell your product or service, and for every referral, or for every product bought, you agree to pay them a fee.

3. Share your knowledge through consulting. Chances are, if you have started a business in something and are even moderately successful, then you have learned quite a bit. Offer to share this knowledge and experience with other businesses that are in need—for a price, of course! For example: If you have a catering business you can offer to teach people how to plan menus, purchase goods, create catering plans, etc.

4. Offer e-courses and material. Take a deeper dive in the consulting arena and use the information you have learned

to create informational products that will create passive income on your site. For example: If you are a graphic designer you could offer a bundle of your favorite fonts for download, templates of client pitches, or whatever else someone would find helpful. Still unsure, of what types of products to market? Think of the things you would have loved to know when you just started out.

5. Teach a class. Yet another way to profit off of your learning curve and experience is by teaching a class or seminar. This can be a great way to build your following while generating revenue.

6. Speak your piece! Conferences, trade shows, companies, and events are always in need of speakers, and if you know what you are talking about they are also willing to pay you well!

Empowering Scripture

"For we are God's handiwork, created in Christ Jesus to do good works, which God prepared in advance for us to do."

Ephesians 2:10

Write now! Don't forget the ideas you have while reading this section:_____

_____

_____

_____

_____

_____

_____

_____

_____

_____

_____

_____

_____

_____

_____

_____

_____

_____

_____

BLOCK 5

B.U.S.I.**N̲**.E.S.S.P.E.R.S.O.N.

N̲etwork

BLOCK 5: Network

More than likely, to get to the "next level" there will always be a person who introduces you to a new audience. Just as you have been establishing relationships with your followers, there are many others who have been putting in the same hard work, and access to their networks will become golden opportunities for you. People trust their "expert," so if that expert trusts you, their people will also. It's that simple. Think about it—who do you revere as a guru, boss, or expert, and how much do you trust their advice? If that person said, "Hey, I know someone who can help you with that. Call this number…" would you hesitate to reach out to that person or business being referred? Probably not. Networking is not so much about reaching your client base as it is about reaching peers, thought leaders in your industry and mentors.

Beware! Networking is not just about attending events and growing a massive contact list. It is genuinely about building Quality relationships, developing your skills and growing a true network. Networking is an excellent way to develop communication skills as you continuously introduce your brand and bring awareness to new initiatives or meaningful causes. It is also a valuable way to expand your knowledge, learn from the success of others, attain new clients and tell others about your business.

Keep in mind that networking requires being genuine and authentic, building trust and relationships and seeing how you can help others. Don't forget your purpose! Don't forget your call! Ask yourself what your goals are in participating in networking meetings so that you will pick groups that will help you get what you are looking for. Some meetings are based more on learning, making contacts, and/or volunteering rather than on strictly making business connections. The art of business networking may take some time to master and perfect, but it is worth it as it will help your business grow.

There are so many different benefits to good business networking. These skills have the potential to help generate more referrals while also increasing revenue. Remember, word-of-mouth marketing is responsible for about seventy percent of new business. Some sources will say eighty-five percent! As you build up your contacts and make more acquaintances, more and more people will be talking about your business and be interested in the services you offer. People like to pass good experiences and services on to their own friends and family. However, this is only going to happen if you make a good impression. Networking is creating an in-person experience that gives people a taste of your businesses' vision, mission, culture and values. Everything in the moment of that iconic hand shake is a snap shot of what people are in for if they do business with you and your company. Make each encounter "pop!"

It is a good idea to join networking groups that are registered through industry associations. Joining these groups will help you keep up to date with changes in your industry, and may also get you invited to other more valuable events. Joining networking groups will give you a chance to meet people from a wider range of small to medium-sized businesses. Industry associations may:

- Give you information about your industry (i.e. how changes to legislation will affect your business)
- Provide you with useful resources (i.e. information and programs to help you meet industry standards)
- Run training and education programs
- Organize seminars
- Facilitate networking events
- Manage mentoring programs
- Connect you with other businesses in your industry
- Arrange public relations or advertising activities to promote your industry
- Organize advertising campaigns to educate or persuade the public about issues relevant to your industry
- Lobby on behalf of your industry to influence government policy

At these types of events meet with anyone and everyone, and certainly send a good follow up. If the person you're meeting with can't afford you or isn't a good fit for your services, they may know someone who could be. A quick email is a professional way to let someone know that you valued their time, and also be sure to connect with them on social platforms like LinkedIn. Waiting around for others to reach out to you may stir your anxiety so go ahead and contact them. You may have been at an event hoping to "level up," but for someone else, meeting you was their big break! Consider these connections as sacred and cherished opportunities for all sides.

Building trusting relationships and formal partnerships can take time. There can be tension and competing agendas. Even so, it's worth taking some time to assess the value of the connection and the fit with your organization; especially as you are building brand recognition. Brand awareness is one of the most important benefits of networking. It effectively helps your industry to recognize and remember your brand. The ultimate goal for any successful entrepreneur is to become an influencer in their field. Influencers are individuals with followings and a voice in the industry. They lead and help set the direction for others. Establishing yourself as an influencer does miracles for your reputation and credibility, which directly translates to business success. While there is no proven path to becoming an influencer, connecting with and engaging other influencers is an important part of building a name for yourself.

Becoming a person of influence in your industry can be very rewarding, though the idea of putting yourself in the spotlight can be incredibly uncomfortable. This is not the time for letting self-doubt creep in. Resist getting in the mindset of asking, "Do I know enough? Am I really an expert?" Lean on your faith! Stand on prayer! Shake off those self-limiting thoughts. The power in your networking moment may not be all numbers and stats. By sharing your knowledge and experiences with overcoming obstacles and challenges you will be able to connect and inspire others. You may even positively influence their future decisions. Being an industry influencer in your industry is not about you. It is actually about the people you want to influence or motivate. Put them first. Today, it takes more than being good at what you do to stand out from the crowd. People want to know what you have to offer, but they don't necessarily want you to sell to them. You must have an authentic personal brand—what you stand for and how you are perceived.

Empowering Scripture

"So then we pursue the things which make for peace and the building up of one another."

Romans 14:19

"Without the guidance of good leaders a nation falls. But many good advisers can save it."

Proverbs 11:14

Write now! Don't forget the ideas you have while reading this section:_____

_____

_____

_____

_____

_____

_____

_____

_____

_____

_____

_____

_____

_____

_____

_____

_____

_____

_____

_____

_____

_____

BLOCK 6

B.U.S.I.N.**E.**S.S.P.E.R.S.O.N

Experience & Competence

BLOCK 6: Experience & Competence

Customers and clients, whether businesses or individuals, must be convinced that they can trust you and your business' ability to actually meet their need. Earning this trust is extremely important to establishing yourself. There are many things that help with this:

- Being referred by someone they trust
- Demonstrated experience
- Quality assurance
- Money back guarantees
- Certifications
- Licenses
- Accreditations
- Number of years in business
- Awards and recognition
- Academic Degrees
- Quality staff
- Impressive board members
- Expedient completion time

To be successful, a business must be able to do what it claims to be able to do, and do it well! If a business offers massages, to be competitive, that business owner must consider many things, such as:

- Who is giving the massages and what is their experience?

- Are they licensed?
- Are they trained in the newest techniques?
- What is unique about the service?
- Is the business licensed with the state?
- Are there quality products being used on the clients?
- Is a quality atmosphere created?
- Does the building meet all codes?

In short, the client is judging everything about the business, the product and the services to gauge whether or not to invest their time, money and expectations. Here is the irony—most people make these determinations while viewing a website before they ever step foot in a facility, or speak to an employee, or ask a real person questions about the product. Herein is the challenge for you—how do you communicate your experience and convey your competence when you haven't even had the opportunity to engage the potential customer yet? You must be masterful at branding and make sure that every aspect of the advertising reiterates all that the business and team members have to offer.

First impressions are everything! When you are blessed enough, to earn a new client, they must leave the experience feeling that you fixed their problem. The idea of creating services or products that help your clients to the extent that they no longer need you may seem to conflict with the purpose of business. However, if a person comes to your workshop for a cooking class, they need to build enough self-efficacy in their time with you that they feel they can cook when they go back home. If a person takes swimming lessons, the business offering the lessons should not desire for that person to always need them. At some point, the mark of a quality experience is that the person learned how to swim and no longer needs the service.

Entrepreneurs should want their work efforts to be more than the passing of time or making a buck. They should be interested in providing great services or products that truly improve their clients' lives. It is one thing to "think" that you are helpful, and another to actually "be" helpful. Most professions have developed *Standards of Practice* which define and outline requirements for competent service. The fact that a person loves eating does not make them a chef. The point is: No matter how persuasive that person is, without proof of skills and expertise, you would not want them to merely be practicing on you.

When clients come to you for help, they want to know that you have knowledge, skills, and abilities that are backed with both training and experience. They also want to know that they can be confident you will not harm them, but instead meet accepted standards of practice for your field. It is your responsibility to ensure that you know those standards of practice and actually follow them! If you are unsure or do not feel confident in a specific area, you can improve through various means including self-study, completing courses or workshops, setting up mentee arrangements, or taking on internship assignments. Unconscious incompetence means that you do not know what you do not know, and you cannot teach what you have no knowledge of. There are blind spots that can jeopardize your personal and professional life. Because of this, it is important to have honest professional peers who will not only point these things out, but also help in figuring out how to overcome them.

Although there are no rules about how much experience a person should have when starting a business, you should find out how different types of experience can help. You will likely realize you have more relevant experience than you thought. Having worked in a similar field or industry of your new business project will, of course, mean that you have a greater understanding of that market and the way things work. This should help you identify customers, marketing strategies and opportunities for growth. Here is a good place to stop and ponder, "What experience do I have? What competencies can I advertise?"

Being experienced may also mean having access to a ready list of contacts, which can be really useful when you are trying to find suppliers, advice or other people to work with. Experience can also give you more confidence in a certain area than if you have never done anything like it before—you have a better idea of what to expect and can foresee problems more clearly. If you are planning to enter an industry with no prior experience, think about whether you would benefit from first finding a job in that field for a year or so to build your experience. You might even want to consider an apprenticeship. Alternatively, talk to as many people as you can in that industry, read trade magazines and books, and anything else you can get your hands on to give you a deeper understanding of that sector.

This is important—Just because a person has not run a business before, does not mean they do not have experience in business. A person learns things from every job they have ever had. They should have observed the most efficient processes, how to speak to people, problems to avoid, etc. Even if there were many challenges, as much can be learned from former mistakes as successes. Try writing out the key skills you picked up from each job, what you thought worked about the way the business was run and what really frustrated you. Take careful note of what frustrated or discouraged customers, suppliers and other staff at previous jobs. This gives you the basis for figuring out the best way to run your own business. It's all relevant—you likely know how to make a profit, handle stock, handle buyers and close a sale.

Now that you have identified skills you already possess, think about what skills you need to enhance or acquire. Apprenticeships and vocational courses are a huge help. They provide job experience and "know how." The next step is formal training and development. There is a large range of certified business courses and development programs you can complete to ensure you get your knowledge to a certain standard before embarking on a startup. These are by no means necessary to run a business, but they can help you improve areas you feel weak in, or give you a better grounding in overall business and management theory. Remember, depending on your field, if you are actually hands-on in providing the services and not just running the business, certain training may be a legal requirement. Training programs can also help you structure a business and make sure you account for all the groundwork necessary. You can choose a single course on one topic, or a longer more intensive program lasting anywhere from a few months to years. Be sure to examine the program content very carefully before committing. Make sure it is going to give you the exposure and skills that it advertises. If you have already completed a degree, consider professional development courses. These courses usually fit around working hours, as they may only be one day long, a three-day seminar, a one-week modular, or online and self-paced. Note: Pay attention to the experience and competence of the institution or company providing the training, as well as the individual experience of the instructor. Be sure to compare pricing. You by no means need a degree to run a business, but if you are aiming to become a fully-fledged entrepreneur, you would benefit from the advanced knowledge offered by a degree in Business, Leadership, Entrepreneurship, or your specialty area. Knowing standards of practice and developing your expertise will provide many benefits for you and your clients, increasing confidence all the more.

Empowering Scripture

"Study to shew thyself approved unto God, a workman

that needeth not to be ashamed, rightly dividing the word

of truth."

2 Timothy 2:15

Write now! Don't forget the ideas you have while reading this section:_____

_____

_____

_____

_____

_____

_____

_____

_____

_____

_____

_____

_____

_____

_____

_____

_____

_____

_____

_____

_____

BLOCK 7

B.U.S.I.N.E.**S**.S.P.E.R.S.O.N

Specify the Market

BLOCK 7: Specify the Market

Practically every marketing and branding expert will strongly suggest picking a niche for your business. (This was discussed in Block Two.) Yet, there are many entrepreneurs and business owners out there who are quite generic in their marketing messages. They are willing to work with anybody to solve any problem, as long as there is a chance of getting a paying client. The truth is, that person is actually losing more of their ideal clients by not declaring a niche and specifying their market. Why? This is because there is no area of expertise established. People are more likely to think of you every time they meet someone with a particular problem if you position yourself as an expert who fixes or heals that particular problem. For example: if someone needs an all-natural vegan cake for a wedding, it makes more sense to refer them to the bakery that specializes in all-natural vegan ingredients, than to refer them to any general bakery to ask if they can meet the need. That specialty bakery may not get as many general orders, but they get ALL of the orders for vegan requests. There are countless bakeries who are in competition for general orders, but this specialty bakery likely runs the show when it comes to vegan needs. Consequently, this specialty bakery has specified their market and can more intentionally designate advertising and marketing budgets to their ideal customer.

Knowing the specific market for a business also means not having to compete by always lowering prices. Your specialty is of utmost value to your clientele, and therefore, it may be considered priceless; allowing you to increase your fee instead! Creating a target market involves three key steps:

- Identify your niche. What is your specialty?
- Articulate what compels customers to buy from you. Why is your product or service better?
- Take the risks out of purchases. Explain how your customer will get exactly what they want.

Identifying a target market implies clearly defining a specific group of prospects who you believe to be most willing to purchase your product or service. That does not mean you will never sell to anyone else, but that you will focus your marketing message towards that narrowly defined group. If you are selling to individuals, identify who they are in terms of nationality, geographical location, gender, age, marital status, income, children, interests, hobbies, reading habits, leisure activities, etc. This allows you to start thinking about what to talk to them about, where to place your marketing messages, why they will buy from you, how they will buy from you, how often, how much they may spend, where you will find them and exactly when they are most likely to buy. With this clearly defined it is much easier to design your marketing strategy, materials, budget, schedule and competitive edge.

For most businesses, what they sell can be bought from someone else or another provider just as easily. So they must ask, "Why me?" This is where the unique selling proposition (USP), comes into play (as discussed in Block Four). Your USP is made up of three elements:

- What is different and unique about you, your business, your product, or your service? Ex: *The Chewy Cookie* bakery offers a baking area for the public to bake thier own cookies with their storebought dough. Perfect for small parties and tour groups.

- What do you excel at? Ex. Even though *The Chewy Cookie* offers a variety of baked goods, they specialize in sugar-free cookies, especially chewy recipes.

- What elements of the things mentioned above are of great value to your customers? Ex: Customers of The Chewy Cookie are cookie lovers who enjoy fun family friendly outings, and who may prefer sugar-free cookies.

Stop! Ask yourself right now, can you visualize *The Chewy Cookie*? Did you imagine those baking stations and cookie parties while reading those examples? This place actually exists in your mind and is like no other place you'll ever visit. How did this happen? The unique products and services made it stand out. This is how you must market your business—by highlighting what makes you different! Take these amazing attributes and turn them into advantages for your target market. Think, "Why would a customer choose my product or service?" Then, go ahead and ask them! Either in conversation, in an email survey, via a suggestion box in the business location, etc. consider asking, "What is so great about this place or this item? Why was it that you chose to buy from us today?" Taking these steps can really help someone to develop a pretty good idea of who their customer is and what is important to them.

Empowering Scripture

"Nevertheless, each person should live as a believer in whatever situation the Lord has assigned to them, just as God has called them. This is the rule I lay down in all the churches."

1 Corinthians 7:17

Write now! Don't forget the ideas you have while reading this section:_____

_____

_____

_____

_____

_____

_____

_____

_____

_____

_____

_____

_____

_____

_____

_____

_____

_____

_____

_____

BLOCK 8

B.U.S.I.N.E.S.**S**.P.E.R.S.O.N

Summarize the Competition

BLOCK 8: Summarize the Competition

Take a look at what your competitors are offering. Check out their website, brochures and advertisements. Even anonymously buy from them. Can you offer something substantially different that is of great value to your customers? Almost all businesses have to face stiff competition with their business rivals in virtually any market today. Having an advantage over them is not enough to guarantee you can sustain your position on the competitive ground. An ongoing analytical survey of the market and its volatility is required to keep you updated and informed of the need for improving the quality of your product and ensuring the superiority of your service. Neglecting to keep your eye on the changing climate of the market creates an unacceptable risk.

No matter how you advertise, there are going to be those who see it or hear it and will just not be prospects for what you are selling. That is fine! You need to make sure that your message is directed for, and targeted only to, those who are qualified prospects for your business. You need to know exactly who it is that buys what you're selling and then talk directly to those people. For example: If a person is in the market for a new vehicle, there is a good chance they will be paying attention to every single television commercial, actively listening to radio commercials, reading newspaper ads, or clicking "Learn More" on social media posts. What is a salesman to do? They must become experts in knowing what the competition is offering, and then be better. A person in need of a mobile catering truck isn't interested in the new Ferrari on sale at the local dealership; and honestly, the Ferrari dealership isn't competition! If you are selling catering trucks you need to know who else is selling mobile kitchens in your target demographic and compete. Create ads and marketing strategies that reach the caterer, the chef, and the restaurant that wants to start serving at park festivals and on college campuses.

Some advertisers feel like they need to put something catchy, cute, weird, sexy, colorful or bold in their ads to make sure that every person on earth pays attention to the ad. Then, they figure, if everyone is looking, then they have a better chance of selling to more people. There is a real trap in doing your advertising this way–a trap that you need to avoid. And here it is again: when you try to speak to everybody, your message gets diluted to the point where it says nothing to anybody. This is called the "Tigger" syndrome. Tigger is a character from the cartoon, Winnie the Pooh. He is a hyperactive tiger who has a spring for a tail and his talent is bouncing. He is the best bouncer of all, but his main goal in life is NOT to excel at bouncing, but rather to be liked by everyone else so he always tries to do what everyone else is doing so they will like him. Someone asks him if he can ice skate to which he replies, "That's what TIGGERS do best!" He goes on to crash into a tree and ruin everyone's fun. Someone asks him if he can climb trees to which he replies, "That's what TIGGERS do best!" Then he promptly gets stuck at the top of the tree. He does this time and time again until finally, demoralized, he realizes that his efforts are best spent and most appreciated when perfecting his own talent–bouncing!

You might be wondering what importance this reference has in business, but would you believe that there are Tiggers in the business world? These are people who start out doing what they love best but change under pressure to become what they are not, and of course, they ultimately fail. They try to be a Jack of All Trades! They offer every service you need and excel at none. There are a lot of different situations. But you cannot try to sell to all of them at once! You have got to make your message focused, like a laser beam, in order to effectively reach your real target market and rise above your competition.

Your competitive advantage is what gives you the edge over a competitor. It is a product feature or attribute, which is superior to that of the others on the market. Or, it might be a service that you are able to perform better than your competitors. Regardless of what it happens to be, that competitive edge can be exploited in order to attract new customers, and can also become a catalyst to drive sales. However it is vitally important, that this advantage be clearly and effectively communicated to clients. The message ought to be specific, and should be communicated at every opportunity. The following are tips on how to communicate your competitive advantage:

1. Develop a positioning statement: The statement should be compelling, accurate, descriptive and carefully crafted in order to grab the attention of the target audience. The purpose of the statement is to underline the differences between your product, and that of your competitors, as well as to outline the benefits of your product or service. This will ensure that there is no doubt in the mind of the target audience, the value that your product is expected to deliver.

2. Traditional marketing campaigns: These can be in the form of television commercials, radio promotions, or similar outlets. Be sure to include the positioning statement, or a tag line that the customer can identify and easily recall. Ensure that the campaigns appeal to customers' interests and needs, and are designed to elicit a positive response.

3. Social Media: Whether you use your business website, blogs, Twitter, or Facebook, social networking is a powerhouse of networking and advertising. Social platforms are great for communicating what you do or sell. There is no better tool to help you get word out about your competitive advantage that compares in affordability and ease of use.

Because of the many special interest groups and the public catalog of friends and followers, social platforms have the best avenue for reaching target populations for virtually no cost, and allowing you to build brand recognition and market familiarity with your competitive advantage. (There is more about this in Block Nine.)

In short, consumers will be willing to buy your product if they know about it, and if there is a clear difference in terms of cost or value from the others being offered on the market! If you are able to establish that you can deliver a product of distinction and superior value, a better service, or a great product at a lower cost, then that will lead to more sales. (High five!) Many companies who do not hold a competitive advantage have often recognized the wisdom of investing in resources to create one. Innovation and creativity can go a long way in ensuring the longevity of a company. Customers do not mind paying premium price for products of better value. Having a competitive advantage is one sure way of attracting new customers and increasing profits.⬚

Empowering Scripture

"For it is God's will that by doing good you should silence the ignorant talk of foolish people."

1 Peter 2:15

"He who walks blamelessly and does what is right and speaks truth in his heart; who does not slander with his tongue and does no evil to his neighbor, nor takes up a reproach against his friend; in whose eyes a vile person is despised, but who honors those who fear the Lord; who swears to his own hurt and does not change; who does not put out his money at interest and does not take a bribe against the innocent. He who does these things shall never be moved."

Psalm 15:1-5

Write now! Don't forget the ideas you have while reading this section:_____

_____

_____

_____

_____

_____

_____

_____

_____

_____

_____

_____

_____

_____

_____

_____

_____

_____

_____

_____

_____

BLOCK 9

B.U.S.I.N.E.S.S.**P.**E.R.S.O.N

Promoting & Marketing

Now that you have a business with a product or service to sell, it is time to tell the world about it. Everything you've learned about niches and target markets must be put into promotional vehicles to get the word out so you can reach your revenue goals. If you've already done this and you're at the point where nothing you have done has produced profit, go back to your business concept and marketing plan and revise it! Pray for clarification. Observe the strategies of competitors in your market and find out what is wrong. Listen: If marketing is not in your skill set, hire a marketing consultant that will market your business and make key suggestions. This is not the time to be defensive and hold your business hostage because you want to be able to say, "I did it all by myself." If you are not adept in this area get help, or strap down and make the commitment to learn what you need to know to be a good steward over your vision. You can utilize the following methods to get started:

- Google Alerts: Email updates of the latest relevant Google results based on a choice of query or topic. This will help you stay current and know the latest changes in your niche.

- Google AdWords: A keyword advertising system in which ads appear as "sponsored links" on the Google results pages as well as the results pages of Google's partners, such as AOL and Ask.com. The advertiser chooses keywords and a short one or two line text ad, which is displayed on the results pages when the ad keywords match up with the search keywords. Statistics of monthly searches are also provided.

- Google Analytics: A free service offered by Google that generates detailed statistics about the visitors to a website as a means of gathering information regarding your product and potential customers.

Why these Google tools? Because Google is, by far, the most popularly accessed search engine which makes it the forerunner in data collection which you can access and use to better strategize promotions and advertisements. After hiring a marketing consultant and utilizing these marketing tools (or similar solutions), if business still does not ramp up, CHANGE YOUR CONCEPT! This does not mean you should set aside your original ideas or mission, it just means that you should spice it up. The choices you make at this point determine how far you will go. If you are in business and you are not profitable, YOU MUST CHANGE something! Think of a *feasibility test* as a reality check for your business idea. The goal of conducting a feasibility test is to prove to yourself and your team of investors that there is relative certainty of your product or service being successful within your industry. A feasibility test should be designed to be as low-cost as possible and should revolve around creating a *Minimum Viable Product* (MVP), or a core proof of concept that communicates the most simple and basic value propositions of your product or service. An MVP should demonstrate:

- The product your business will offer
- The customer you will target
- Your value proposition
- How you will get the product to its intended users; your distribution channels.

In essence, your value proposition is what makes customers choose you instead of the competition. It's part marketing, part operations, and part strategy. Your value proposition is the foundation of your competitive advantage. On a subconscious level, customers will compare the value proposition of your company against those of your competitors when deciding where to take their business. With that in mind, here are a few things to remember when writing your value proposition:

- Keep it short and uncluttered. Your value proposition explains why customers should buy from you. If you cannot sum it up in ten words or less, chances are you will not be able to execute it, either.
- Be precise. Your customers have specific needs; your value proposition should offer targeted solutions.
- This is about your customer, not you. Your value proposition should discuss only what matters to your customers and the value you can bring to them.

- Value comes in numerous forms. Money, time, convenience and superior service are a few of the ways you can help deliver value to your customers.

Marketing and advertising will be among the biggest keys to sustained success. Owning a business and not embarking on any advertising campaigns can be detrimental to profitability. It is of utmost importance. Without doing this you simply cannot expect anyone else to know that you or your business even exists. Getting your name out there is absolutely essential. After all, when you market your business well, you will keep your business at the front of the public's consciousness, and will keep them coming back to you. However, understanding that advertising is important is not quite the same thing as understanding the best and most effective ways to advertise, and for this reason, it is worthwhile to take a closer look at some of the best things you can do to advertise for your business.

In the advertising and marketing world there are a variety of advertising mediums available—the options are literally endless. For example: Outdoor advertising has certainly grown in popularity over the past few years and it is no wonder why! This type of advertising provides more exposure and coverage than any other form of advertising or marketing if you are a business operating in a particular area. Having focused outdoor advertisements can simply work wonders for your company. You should consider the following forms of outdoor advertising for your business: street pole signs, bus stops, billboards, banner ads, street name posters, or signage at events. New-preneurs need to be realistic about advertising budgets, so look for effective low-cost solutions. If you are armed with the right marketing essentials you cannot help but succeed in attracting new prospects and bringing in more business. Spend some time on getting your marketing toolkit in place according to the items below:

- A plan and a budget: Getting a plan that will support you for years to come is essential to keeping you on track. It does not need to be as thick as *War and Peace*, but it does need to be written down, clearly communicated to your team and acted on day by day—even when business is booming.

- A great product or service: Advertising your business has no point if the customers do not want, value or love what you have to offer. Make sure you do your research and listen to your customers (or potential customers) before sending your product out to the market.

- A professional brand: A brand is much more than a logo. It encompasses everything people see, hear, think and feel about your business. Invest up-front in developing a brand that stands out from the crowd. It will save you money and heartache in the long run.

- Powerful marketing materials: Your business card, sales brochures, sales letters, website, signage, uniforms and even car decals, can speak volumes about your business. Make sure they look professional and appealing at all times.

- An elevator pitch: In the course of marketing your business you will get asked thousands of times, "What do you do?'" Do not make the mistake of boring the poor person who asked the question! Make sure you have a fun, interesting and memorable pitch ready at all times—and be able to deliver it in the time it takes to travel a few floors in an elevator.

- A brilliant website: Your website must attract attention and give value to those who visit. Use it as a tool to retain and keep in touch with existing customers as well as for enticing new customers. The online world can be very scary to many small-business owners; but, if you do not embrace it, you may find yourself unable to compete.

- A simple database: The backbone of all good marketing is about building a solid database of past, present and future customers (prospects) so you can keep in touch and communicate regularly via e-newsletters, emails, texts, etc. This is the tool that allows you to take advantage of *automation*—when people who engage your ads or emails are automatically funneled into a series of follow-up emails with additional ads, testimonials, upcoming event invitations, or even special discounts and offers.

You do not need to spend buckets of money on marketing. Creativity and a bit of gumption to do something different from everyone else in the market can be the difference between business success and business failure. The following are just a few of countless ideas on how to market a business:

- Attend networking events. It is not what you know, but who you know. Gas discussed in Block five, get out there and network—meet and greet. You can never have too many people learning about your business, even if they do not end up as customers.

- Sponsor a local event or charity. It really does make you feel good to support your community, and everyone benefits— you, your staff, your customers, and the people you sponsored.

- Manage your public relations. Getting your name up in lights on TV and radio, and in newspapers and magazines is not as hard as you think "IF" you have a story worth telling! This takes you back to your initial reason for stepping into this endeavor and what problem you want to solve. Tell your story, give your testimony, and let the world know why your product ro service is the answer they've been waiting for.

- Use social media. Using social-networking sites like Facebook, Twitter and LinkedIn, producing your own videos for YouTube, or writing your own blog are creative methods of letting people know about you and your business.

- Host seminars and events. Hosting your own events and inviting your best customers and some of their friends is a great way to get to know people, connect at a personal level and build quality business relationships.

- Become a public speaker. Whether public speaking is a fear or not, invest in developing this area! Hone your skills and become a great and entertaining speaker. It is a fabulous way to demonstrate your expertise and generate new business inquiries from those who attend your events.

Most small business owners, especially new-preneurs just starting out, do not have lots of money for marketing. While the old adage, "you need to spend money to make money," is true, you can generate new business without having to spend big bucks. Try a few of these tactics for a start:

- Focus on relationship-building marketing strategies such as building alliances with other businesses, or by calling old customers, friends and people you once worked with who may be willing to help you by sharing your ads to their own networks and followings.

- Find people who are prepared to help you with marketing on a commission basis. This is *Affiliate Marketing*, and you can register your products or services for affiliates to promote for you and generate leads.

- Reach out to university students who are studying marketing and might need hands-on experience to fulfill internship requirements.
- Develop a marketing mastermind group with other small-business owners for the purpose of sharing low-cost marketing ideas and referring each other business.
- Sharpen your own online marketing skills, learn how to use Google AdWords, write blogs, and market yourself on the social media sites by boosting posts and split-testing.
- Promote your business on free online directories and publish your articles on other websites with links to your site.
- Use *Search Engine Optimization* (SEO) to reach the people. SEO describes the key words and phrases programed to be associated with your website that help it to be found easier by those searching for the type or products or services you offer.

The fact of the matter is that every single business, business owner and entrepreneur in a Chirstian vocation has success within reach. All it takes is for them to recognize that success can be achieved and to have the pure determination to make it happen. Once this realization is made it will only be a matter of time before they are winning the entrepreneur shuffle!

Empowering Scripture

"My mouth will tell of your righteous acts, of your deeds of salvation all the day, for their number is past my knowledge. With the mighty deeds of the Lord God I will come; I will remind them of your righteousness, yours alone. O God, from my youth you have taught me, and I still proclaim your wondrous deeds. So even to old age and gray hairs, O God, do not forsake me, until I proclaim your might to another generation, your power to all those to come."

Ephesians 2:10

Write now! Don't forget the ideas you have while reading this section:_____

_____

_____

_____

_____

_____

_____

_____

_____

_____

_____

_____

_____

_____

_____

_____

_____

_____

_____

_____

_____

BLOCK 10

B.U.S.I.N.E.S.S.P.**E.**R.S.O.N

Ethics & Integrity

BLOCK 10: Ethics & Integrity

In the search of success and wealth, many people tend to forget that it would be impossible to get to where they would like to be (and stay there) without God's grace. Some people forget that God has standards of righteousness that are expected to be implemented; even in their businesses. As an entrepreneur, you should know the importance of honoring God in all that you do. To safe guard your business from making any oversights in this area, be sure that in addition to searching for success and wealth that you are seeking to glorify God and transform lives. This becomes the measure of your integrity and should be reflected in your vision and mission statements.

Remember, you are in business to fix a problem. Be sure to remember the reason why you started offering your product or service in the first place and its potential to relieve someone's burden. Although money is important and could be a core reason for starting a business, it shouldn't be your "only" reason. Once making money becomes the "only" reason for doing business, that is the beginning of failure. If you find that you've arrived to a place of being overly focused on making money, and you've compromised your character and principles in doing so, you can stop and turn things around. Pray! Put in the effort to change the current situation: go through your business plans and concepts to determine what needs to be changed.

Pay tithes and sow seeds into good ground. Many people, though they identify themselves as Christians, still do not understand the concept of paying tithes. Some think, "Why does God need money?" Or, "What difference will my money make to God?" If this is a practice that you have questions about or need further information on, schedule time to talk it over with your pastor or a ministry leader. As an individual, set out to give a minimum of ten percent of your earnings to God on a regular basis. You can also have a percentage of your business' revenue to be allocated toward this form of giving. There are numerous ways to accomplish this: donations directly to a church or faith based organization, charitable causes, foundations, etc. Most importantly, once you start, do not stop! Allow this to become a part of the fabric of your business culture and values. The rewards are eternal.

Paying bills is another matter of ethics and integrity. Satisfy payables on time! Note: When you do not pay bills early or on-time, what was once a small balance quickly becomes more than you budgeted for. Pay your vendors responsibly to avoid problems and to maintain an open door for future negotiations. As a new-preneur, you are just starting to build your business credit and financial portfolio. When the time comes to scale your company, expand, or upgrade, you want to have great financial relationships with creditors, lenders, and vendors that respect you, and what you've built, and who will help you to reach your goals. Proper reporting and record keeping can work miracles for maintaining ethical practices.

Remember, entrepreneurship for the believer is *Christian Vocation*. Stick to your mission! Set out to do what was promised originally. Most businesses that dwindle and fade off the scene do so because they strayed from their initial vision and purpose. It is similar to political campaigning where things are promised to voters and after that representative is elected, none of it gets done. It is frustrating and lowers trust. Deliver! Give your customer what they paid for and more. If you advertise that delivery will be in thirty minutes or less, make sure deliveries are executed on time. If your bar of soap is guaranteed to last three months, make sure it lasts. How you manage your deliverables is important to building brand recognition, brand trust, and return customers.

Furthermore, be mindful of the people you work with. You are in the "people" business and it is important to maintain a healthy work environment and good working relationships. This includes co-founders, executives, board members, employees, volunteers, vendors and of course customers. Basically, everyone! There is no room for harassment, belittling or manipulation anywhere, especially within Christian vocation. Treat people with respect and dignity. Be intentional about creating avenues to receive confidential communications and even suggestions from your team, and make sure that everyone—from the janitor, to the copywriter, to the CEO—feel valued by you and your business. Being considerate of feedback and valuing the team's input does not mean that you have to be a pushover and neglect your own plans. However, there is a level of performance that money cannot buy and salary cannot access. It is a level of performance that is only accessed when a person is convinced that their effort and contribution is genuinely appreciated and sincerely valued. Never forget that your team plays an important role in the growth of your business, and most times, work more than you do. In fact, help them take the first step in pursuing their own dreams and business plans. Be their stepping stone, helping them to get to where they truly want to be. There is something transformational about empowering team members. They transform your vision and you inspire theirs.

Lastly, the importance of good customer service cannot be overemphasized. There are a lot of businesses that should be grateful to have customers, but instead treat people like they are doing them a favor. Treat your customers like they are the reason why your business exists. Why? Because they are! Even if customers are rude, smother them with kindness. Never be defensive or argumentative with customers in person, by phone or online even if you are right! It will make you seem petty and those people will never return.

Empowering Scripture

"But remember the LORD your God, for it is he who gives you the ability to produce wealth, and so confirms his covenant, which he swore to your ancestors, as it is today."

Deuteronomy 8:18

"Do nothing out of selfish ambition or vain conceit. Rather, in humility value others above yourselves, not looking to your own interests but each of you to the interests of the others."

Philippians 2:3-4

Write now! Don't forget the ideas you have while reading this section:_____

_____

_____

_____

_____

_____

_____

_____

_____

_____

_____

_____

_____

_____

_____

_____

_____

_____

_____

BLOCK 11

B.U.S.I.N.E.S.S.P.E.**R**.S.O.N

Risks & Rewards

Entrepreneurial ventures are a vital rprt of the economy. The potential exists to fulfill dreams and become financially independent. No matter how humble the beginnings, over time, entrepreneurial businesses can grow into fortified powerhouses. In contrast, there are businesses that showed promise and great potential for success that ended up folding and dissolving. The reality is that entrepreneurship is risky business. You need to be sure of what you can afford to invest and what you can afford to lose. Some people are building their business with discretionary income, which is the amount of income that a household or individual has to invest, save or spend after taxes and necessities are paid. However, for many people just starting out, they may be repurposing and reallocating money that should be paying for necessities. Some people risk it all.

As an entrepreneur in a Christian vocation, even calculating risks is a matter of stewardship. Especially when the risk extends beyond money to decisions that can impact friends, family or one's faith. How much can you *afford* to risk? This question speaks to financial investment. How much are you *willing* to risk? This question speaks to everything else like effort, hope, relationship capital, status, etc. You need to know, because without the proper planning, foresight and safeguards, this level of pressure can leave someone feeling anxious or hopeless; over-confidant or depressed. Large amounts of funding do not guarantee success. Management and other skills may be lacking. The following case studies highlight the various risks and rewards that some entrepreneurs experience (Names are fictional). Discuss these possibilities with a colleague or business partner and give serious consideration to the likelihood of them happening in your own life. Observe your own reflections and gauge whether or not you're willing to take those risks, and then think critically about measures that can help control these outcomes.

When Everything Goes Wrong

Eric was in his late forties when an entrepreneurial opportunity presented itself. He was an accountant by profession and in a senior position at a medium-sized firm. A new franchise in the automotive industry was offered to him in another town. The opportunity was too good to ignore. Eric considered this an answer to his prayers and an open door from God. He resigned, sold his house and took the money to start the business. The franchise did not turn out to be what was promised. The franchisor was not very honest and Eric was not an entrepreneur at heart. He was passionate about cars, but not about the more technical aspects. In the end, the following potential risks became reality and it had serious conseᵈuences.

- Social risk. When Eric and his wife left town they left behind their "village" and support structure, their home church, and their circle of friends. He worked long hours to build the business. The regular and pleasant social weekend get-togethers were something of the past. Their teenage daughter also had serious problems adjusting that they found difficult to cope with.

- Financial risk. Eventually the business collapsed and Eric was declared bankrupt. At this stage he was in his early fifties.
- Career risk. Eric resigned from a good job with a good pension fund. When everything turned sour he tried to go back to his old firm. There were no vacancies. He accepted a lower paid job as an operational manager.
- Psychological risk. Eventually too many things went wrong with Eric. He divorced, is very bitter today, and often comments that he'll have to "work till the day he dies."
- Spiritual risk. Eric began doubting whether or not this was God's plan at all, and if it was, he questioned God's love for him and his family to let him go through such a difficult situation. Though they had returned to their hometown, he was distant from his church family and spiritual leaders because of having moved away for so long. There were new younger leaders in the church that he didn't know and he found it hard to confide in them.

Is It Worth It?

Jasmine was in her mid-thirties when she and her partners had the opportunity to do a management buy-out of the manufacturing company that they worked for. Over the last seven years they turned the company around from making a loss to a company that is doing exceptionally well. Outsiders would say that this is the ideal situation to be in. Jasmine is experiencing the following:

- Financial reward. Jasmine became a multi-mllionaire. She purchased land to be passed down to her children as an inheritance, and she funded a new toddler day-care facility and a primary school at her local church. She always lived within her means, and she and her family can easily sustain a good living without her having to work another day of her life.

Unfortunately, Jasmine also sees herself as being trapped in a "catch-22" situation. She feels that the price she pays for the financial rewards is too high. She began expressing the following negative impacts on her life:

- Social risks. She spent so much time out of the country that she grew apart from her friends and family. She feels she was not there for her closest friend whose father passed away while she was out on a business trip. She also feels that her children are growing up and she is not there to experience it.

- Psychological risks. Jasmine finds it difficult to balance the work situation and her personal life. At this stage she has a serious problem with depression. Fortunately, her business partners support her exceptionally well and they have formulated a plan for all of them to exit the business in the near future.

The Fruits Of Success

Marc is a serial entrepreneur who started his first business in his early twenties two decades ago. He is very ambitious, made several mistakes and went bankrupt twice. Six years ago he started a business in a niche area of property development. He has an absolute passion for this line of business and in a short period became extremely successful. He thoroughly enjoys his success and believes that all the risk-taking and hard work was worthwhile. He experiences his rewards as follows:

- Financial rewards. Marc is worth several million dollars and he used enough of this money to give him a passive income that affords him and his family a life of luxury. He also makes regular contributions to foundations that he feels passionately about and is helping to change people's lives. Marc is giving a large proportion of his time and money to endorsing and drawing greater support for charities.
- Social rewards. Marc was always a very social person and managed to keep his social life intact. Today he is enjoying much of his social activities with friends on overseas trips and at his holiday farm and beach house.

- Independence rewards. Marc always enjoyed being his own boss. He often said that he would rather sleep in a park than work for somebody else. In the end, his attitude and determination paid off.
- Growth rewards. On a personal level Marc used the opportunity to grow as a person. He learned to fly, did a lot of self-study to improve himself, and people respect him from all walks of life.

These case studies personified various risks and rewards of pursuing entrepreneurship. The following are additional possibilities to consider:

Additional Risks

1. Getting Paid. The income of the business would determine whether the entrepreneur gets paid or not. The entrepreneur does not have the luxury of an assured paycheck like others with employment. If the business does not make profit, any salary to the entrepreneur would have to come from prior revenue, or funds set aside to cover salary. Either way, this situation decreases the business' financial security—a practice that can lead to bankruptcy.

2. Sporadic Income. The start-up entrepreneur may not have enough sales to provide steady income. His or her income may fluctuate from day to day or from month to month. For these reasons, start-up entrepreneurs are usually advised to

save at least enough to cover six months of expenses and income needs as part of their financial planning.

3.   Having Security. Unlike people in paid employment who may have medical, dental and vision benefits as well as a retirement savings account backed by their employer, the entrepreneur has to plan for his or her own insurance and retirement security. Before moving from paid employment to full-time entrepreneurship, it is important that aspiring entrepreneurs add, as part of their financial planning, solutions for medical coverage, life insurance and retirement security.

Additional Rewards

1.   Passion. One of the greatest joys of entrepreneurship is working daily on your life's passion. When your work and daily pursuits are in the realm of your true heart's desires, it results in work done with enthusiasm, appetite and hunger.

2.   Hours. One of the immediate benefits of entrepreneurship is having control of your time. Though the beginning stages may be rough, the ability to set your own schedule for your work and business is a reward of priceless value.

3.   Location. Where you live and work are key factors of personal satisfaction. Entrepreneurship may allow you to avoid long distance commuting or traffic, and to choose between virtual web-based work, or even mobile offices

where you do business between multiple meeting locations and co-op work spaces.

Running your own business full-time can be amazing experience. However, it is very important to contemplate all details objectively to make sure that it fits your personality and risk profile, especially if you envision very rapid growth. It is not the time to hyper-spiritualize the process! Yes, faith will do miraculous things in your business endeavors. You are in this to glorify God and provide resources for kingdom initiatives. However, you will need sound practical planning and strategies to reach your goals. Naïve entrepreneurs often tend to believe that sales growth will take care of everything; that they will be able to fund their own growth by generating profits. However, this is rarely the case, for one simple reason: you usually have to pay suppliers before your customers pay you. This cash flow conundrum is the reason so many fast-growing companies have to seek bank financing or equity sales to finance their growth. They are literally growing faster than they can afford to keep up with!

Each type of financing option has different characteristics that you should take into consideration. These characteristics take three primary forms:

• First, there is the amount of control you will have to surrender. An equal partner may demand e?ual control. Venture capitalists often demand significant input into management decisions by, for instance, placing one or more people on your board of directors. Angel investors may be very involved or not involved at all, depending on their personal style. Bankers are likely to offer no advice whatsoever as long as you make payments of principal and interest on time and are not in violation of any other terms of your loan.

• Secondly, you should consider the amount of money needed to help determine the type of financing you need. For example: A standard initial public stock offering wouldn't be any less than several million dollars. Venture capital investors are most likely to invest between two-hundred and fifty thousand to three million. On the other hand, an angel investor may provide between a few thousand and a few hundred thousand dollars.

• The third consideration is cost. This can be measured in various ways such as the terms of interest rates, miscellaneous fees or shares of ownership, as well as in time, application fees, hassle of gathering documentation requirements, impressions on your personal credit, etc.

If you are looking for a bank loan, you will need a business plan that stresses the business' ability to generate sufficient cash flow. Equity investors, especially venture capitalists, must be shown how they can cash out of your company and generate a rate of return they will find acceptable. Whichever method of financing you pursue, make sure you know what you need and how you will pay it back.

Empowering Scripture

"Ship your grain across the sea; after many days you may receive a return. Invest in seven ventures, yes, in eight; you do not know what disaster may come upon the land. If clouds are full of water, they pour rain on the earth. Whether a tree falls to the south or to the north, in the place where it falls, there it will lie. Whoever watches the wind will not plant; whoever looks at the clouds will not reap. As you do not know the path of the wind, or how the body is formed in a mother's womb, so you cannot understand the work of God, the Maker of all things. Sow your seed in the morning, and at evening let your hands not be idle, for you do not know which will succeed, whether this or that, or whether both will do equally well."

Ecclesiastes 11:1-6

Write now! Don't forget the ideas you have while reading this section:_____

_____

_____

_____

_____

_____

_____

_____

_____

_____

_____

_____

_____

_____

_____

_____

_____

_____

_____

_____

_____

_____

BLOCK 12

B.U.S.I.N.E.S.S.P.E.R.<u>S</u>.O.N

<u>S</u>hipping & Fulfillment

BLOCK 12: Shipping & Fulfillment

It's time to deliver! Every product and service must have a mode of delivery and a distribution plan. Imagine the following to be rapid fire questions a funding source may be asking as they are trying to make sure there is a strategy for them to make a return on their investment:

- Are you going to sell directly to consumers (Business to Consumer (B2C)) or supply other businesses (Business to Business (B2B))?

- Will you set up a brick-and-mortar store or facility, sell online, or both?

- Will it be pre-packaged or made to order?

- Will there be employees for handling and shipping?

- Will you use a drop-ship third party to manage orders?

- How long is the waiting period before the customer receives the product or service?

- Will there be an option of expedited delivery?

- Which transport service will deliver orders, or will the company have its own commercial vehicles and drivers?

- How does this impact insurance?

- If this is a service, where will it be provided?

- Will multiple people be serviced at once?

- Is there a money back guarantee if the customer does not like the product or service?

Remember, vision is important if your business is going to do well and grow. The more focused your business concept is, in terms of clearly anticipated solutions and answers to questions like these, the greater the likelihood that you will do good business and attract the best investors and customers.

Matters of logistics can be managed with sufficient pre-planning. As your brand grows and sales increase, you may even find yourself scaling your business to meet global demands. Using outsourcing shipping tactics is beneficial so you can spend more time channeling your energy toward sales. There are three primary ways your business can benefit from outsourcing your warehousing and shipping:

1. You will be able to reach distant markets and customers. It used to be only the big brands that had the world-class logistical management needed to enter international markets. Not any more! Today, ecommerce companies of all sizes benefit from the convenience of intelligent online logistics and fulfillment services. Easy access to such fulfillment services has leveled the playing field for businesses, just as shopping cart software did for ecommerce and the Internet for global accessibility. For example: A company whose products are manufactured and shipped out of North America might consider the Asian market beyond reach. However, using a logistics provider with a warehouse at a shipping hub in Asia makes

infiltrating the market far less risky. That opens up the potential of tapping into an additional customer base. A second example: English-speaking consumers live all over the world, with native-English speakers in strong economies, like Australia, where the e-commerce market exceeds twelve billion dollars annually. In cases where internationalizing your product line (translating packaging, etc. into other languages) is a challenge, working with a fulfillment partner to provide convenient shipping options and advertising to those native-English speakers allows market testing without making huge investments.

2. Outsourcing will reduce customs hassles for international shipments. Sending packages to international customers is tedious and costly! Often, it's a logistical nightmare. Lost shipments, lack of tracking ability, brokerage fees and the unpredictability of delivery times make shipping to customers in other countries a difficult task. As with most business processes, doing things in bulk is advantageous. Sending a large shipment of products through the border once, and dealing with customs and duties without bothering customers about it, is infinitely beneficial. Outsourcing your shipping and fulfillment, especially with a cloud-based service, means that you send the shipment, and pay the brokerage fees, only once. Typically, the first shipment of goods is sent to the warehouse of a fulfillment

company. With customs forms filled out properly, the process is handled faster and there are fewer risks of delay. Once the product arrives in the warehouse, it is inventoried and ready to be sent to customers. Then, when a sale comes in from a customer in that country, the product can be sent directly from that warehouse. The benefits are significant. The unpredictability of customs delays is eliminated, which lowers return rates and increases your margins. Furthermore, shipping costs are lower, allowing you to compete where you otherwise could not.

3. Dream big! See your venture growing to the point of doing business globally between many different countries. You will cut even more costs by storing inventory around the world. Expanding a warehouse or distribution network will be necessary, but it will also incur more expenses which can easily translate to higher costs. Fortunately, there are options that lower the costs while garnering all the benefits. Utilizing a *fulfillment house* increases your coverage, both domestic and international, thereby lowering shipping costs to customers and increasing the viability of a product in any given market. The available storage for inventory is increased, which especially helps with high-growth enterprises and during high-volume sales periods like holidays. In short, the trick to cutting shipping costs is storing inventory closer to your buyers.

Empowering Scripture

"Like clouds and wind without rain

is one who boasts of gifts never given."

Proverbs 25:14

"Some went out on the sea in ships; they were merchants

on the mighty waters. They saw the works of the Lord, his

wonderful deeds in the deep."

Psalm 107:23-24

Write now! Don't forget the ideas you have while reading this section:_____

_____

_____

_____

_____

_____

_____

_____

_____

_____

_____

_____

_____

_____

_____

_____

_____

_____

_____

_____

BLOCK 13

B.U.S.I.N.E.S.S.P.E.R.S.**O.**N

Objectives & Goals

New-preneurs must be cautious about distractions. Especially those with God given visions that have the potential to stir up new resources that can solve world class problems. Not only will the competition yearn for your failure, but there is a real adversary determined to interrupt your progress, discredit your intentions, and make you doubt your purpose. In this process of building a new business one must have an ultimate goal to reach, they must envision how they are going to move forward, and they absolutely must create a strategy to help them actualize success. This is done by creating objectives and goals, and this is how you will know if you are winning the entrepreneur shuffle. Think of it this way, a strategy is simply a decision about how to use resources to solve a problem. It is a choice about what you will or will not do with what you have in order to achieve a goal; and behind every good strategy there are action plans that bring it to life. For example: If the strategy for building brand recognition is to post tips and tricks for consumers in your niche on social media, the action plan behind it would answer the questions, "Which social platforms? How often? Who is doing the posting? How do you identify which tips to share? Will these posts be boosted and acquire advertising costs? If so, what is the budget? How long will the ads be boosted for? What KPIs are in place to know if the posts are working? Etc." Action items are the beginning of a rewarding journey toward fulfilling vision.

An older—and yet very relevant—tool to help with creating objectives and goals is the S.M.A.R.T. method. This approach suggests that goals and action plans should be *Specific, Measureable, Attainable, Relevant* and *Timely*. For example: If your goal is to specifically bring in ten new clients, your strategy may begin with increasing the number of prospects from your target market. This is something that is measureable. You might also include attainable steps like joining a new networking group in your niche, attending more events where your ideal clients will be present, or even being an official sponsor for some of those events; thus making your brand relevant and on the pulse of your industry. It might also include making sure you actually attend the meetings of the new groups you joined by intentionally scheduling time on your calendar, having a plan for talking to at least five new people at each meeting, or spending thirty minutes a week identifying even more events to look into.

Objectives and goals should be realistic and able to fit within your daily schedule; such as calling event organizers to find speaking engagements! They can be flexible, but that does not mean you don't need to have a specific plan, and a serious personal commitment to actually "work" your plan. Unless it's written down and scheduled, or made concrete for you in some other way, a plan becomes just another "nice idea" that you didn't do anything about. So, while your plans can be flexible and change when they are not serving you well in moving toward your goal, you have to make a heartfelt decision to be committed to at least trying to see them through.

Now, when you have given a strategy a good chance to succeed and find it ineffective, it's time to come up with a new strategy. Remember, experimenting is how you learn. Failures are opportunities to examine what happened with a critical eye and to design a new solution that may work better. Whether you're just starting out in business, or relaunching and looking to grow and get ahead in your market, being aware of these universal building blocks is crucial. It allows you to properly focus your attention and do what is absolutely necessary, rather than waste your time investing in things that will damage your chances of success rather than improve them. Of course, all businesses are different. Therefore, as you read on, you should think creatively about ways in which to incorporate these suggestions into your strategy while being critical and making sure you are not neglecting any key areas. All extra work put in now could pay huge dividends in the future.

One of the most important considerations in setting objectives and goals is the level of accountability included. Checks and balances keep you on target. That is especially true if it is used to raise money to finance your company. Donors want to know that their investment is being used for the exact reason it was given. For example: You forecast opening four new locations in the second year of your retail operation. An investor would definitely be concerned if, due to circumstances you could have foreseen, you only open two. They might ask for the money back, or even sue your business for embezzlement and misappropriation of funds. Measures of accountabIllty within your objectives and goals will keep you ethical and focused. The making of a business plan can take on a life of its own—especially for the creative visionary—so thinking clearly about what you include in your plan is a reasonable act of prudence. It is important to remember why you are doing this. Using key phrases from your vision and mission statements to define your goals is wise. Then by establishing metrics, you can assess your performance and progress to recognize immediately if business is succeeding or going off track.

Business objectives and goals are the results a businessperson hopes to achieve and maintain as they run and grow their company. As an entrepreneur, you are concerned not only for the overall "big picture" matters, but also for every single aspect and minute detail. The following are the top ten things you should heve business objectives and goals for.

1. Profitability—Maintaining profitability means making sure that revenue stays ahead of the costs of doing business. Focus on controlling costs in both production and

operations while maintaining the profit margin on products sold.

2. Productivity—Training, new eＱuipment, administrative software, operating systems, etc. all go into company productivity. Your objective should be to provide all of the resources your business and your team needs to remain as productive as possible.

3. Customer Service—Good customer service helps to retain clients and generate repeat revenue. Keeping customers happy should be a primary and foremost objective.

4. Employee Retention—If you have employees, turnover can cost you a lot of money in lost productivity, recruiting, placement agencies, etc. Maintaining a productive and positive employee environment is important.

5. Core Values—Core values are a summary of beliefs held in regard to customer interaction, employee satisfaction, quality commitment, etc. Your business' core values become the objectives necessary to create a positive culture and brand presence within your niche.

6. Growth—Growth is planned based on historical data and future projections. Growth reＱuires the careful use of company resources such as finances and personnel. There must be an expectation to grow and an assessment tool in place to know how much or how little your business has grown at any given time.

7. Maintain Financing—Even a company with good cash flow needs financing solutions in the event that capital is needed for expansion, or for emergencies. Also, maintaining your ability to finance operations means that you can be in a position to take advantage of sudden opportunitites.

8. Change Management—This is the process of preparing your organization for growth and creating processes that effectively deal with a developing marketplace. The objective of change management is to create a dynamic organization that is prepared to meet the challenges of your industry and excel.

9. Marketing—Marketing is more than creating advertising and getting customer input on product changes. It is understanding consumer buying trends, being able to anticipate product distribution needs, and most importantly it is developing business partnerships that help your organization to improve market share.

10. Competitive Analysis—As outlied in Block 8, a comprehensive analysis of the activities of the competition should be an ongoing business objective. Understanding where your products rank in the marketplace helps you to better determine how to improve your standing among consumers while increasing revenue.

Empowering Scripture

"In the morning, LORD, you hear my voice; in the morning,

I lay my requests before you and wait expectantly."

Psalm 5:3

Write now! Don't forget the ideas you have while reading this section:_____

_____

_____

_____

_____

_____

_____

_____

_____

_____

_____

_____

_____

_____

_____

_____

_____

_____

_____

BLOCK 14

B.U.S.I.N.E.S.S.P.E.R.S.O.**N.**

Negotiate Partnerships

BLOCK 14: Negotiate Partnerships

The entrepreneur shuffle can feel, at times, like a lonely pursuit—especially in the beginning stages. However, it doesn't have to be! Negotiating strategic partnerships can be a great solution. There are definitely benefits to partnering with one or more other individuals or businesses who share similar interests and intensions. Benefits include:

- Experience and industry knowledge
- Access to other networks and contacts lists
- Combining resources; both fiscal and human
- Earning referral or affiliate fees
- Extended skill sets and competencies
- Accountability and increased productivity
- Motivation and support

If managed correctly, a partnership can alleviate a lot of stress and give the vision more support. The following are seven forms of partnerships that you should consider.

1. General Partnerships—Two or more co-owners who each have equal power to act as an agent for the partnership. Each partner can be held liable for all debts of the partnership, and for the actions of other partners on behalf of the business.

2. Limited Partnerships—A structure where one or more people can be a general partner and the other(s) be limited partners. A limited partner has no voice in the active

management of the business, which is conducted by the general partner(s). Every limited partner's liability is limited to the capital they contributed to the partnership.

3. Limited Liability Partnerships— These have much more in common with limited liability companies (LLC) than they do other types of business partnerships. With an LLP, partners will receive the same beneficial taxation provided by a general partnership, and will also be shielded from the debts, and liabilities of the business. In addition, every partner in an LLP will be protected from the actions of other partners.

4. Mergers

    a. Conglomerate Merger—A merger between firms that are involved in totally unrelated business activities. There are two types of conglomerate mergers: pure and mixed. Pure conglomerate mergers involve firms with nothing in common, while mixed conglomerate mergers involve firms that are looking for product extensions or market extensions.

    b. Horizontal Merger—A merger occurring between companies in the same industry. Horizontal merger is a business consolidation that occurs between firms who operate in the same space, often as competitors offering the same product or service. Horizontal mergers are common in industries with fewer firms, as competition tends to be higher and the synergies and potential gains in market share are much greater for merging firms in such an industry.

c. Market Extension Mergers—A market extension merger takes place between two companies that deal in the same products but in separate markets. The main purpose of the market extension merger is to make sure that the merging companies can get access to a bigger market and that ensures a bigger client base.

d. Product Extension Mergers—A product extension merger takes place between two business organizations that deal in products that are related to each other and operate in the same market. The product extension merger allows the merging companies to group together their products and get access to a bigger set of consumers. This ensures that they earn higher profits.

e. Vertical Merger—A merger between two companies producing different goods or services for one specific finished product. A vertical merger occurs when two or more firms, operating at different levels within an industry's supply chain, merge operations. Most often the logic behind the merger is to increase synergies created by merging firms that would be more efficient operating as one.

5. Collaboration—This is simply two or more individuals or businesses working together toward shared goals. In this, and the following forms of partnership, the businesses are not connected legally nor do they have any tax responsibilities to each other.

6. Brand Ambassador—Promoting another business brand. This is usually for a commission. As a brand ambassador, the brand you promote should compliment your brand, products and services. However, it is not necessary to have your own business to promote someone else's.

7. Referral Network—Multiple people or businesses all agreeing to promote or feature one another's services to their own networks. Generally persons in this agreement do not offer the same services as the others they are referring.

Partnerships are tricky. As long as all parties are cooperating, it's good for business. However, if one or all parties don't cooperate with one another it can be difficult and threaten one or all businesses involved. Some challenges cannot be anticipated. However, there are some things that, if given proper attention ahead of time, can help to maintain healthy business relationships. The following are things to review and negotiate when setting the parameters of a partnership:

1. Short and long term goals. Make sure you have the same outcomes in mind. Certain partnerships may bring a lot of change. You do not want your business and your team to absorb the impact of all that transition only to find out later that one or all of the other partners had no plan on staying in it for an extended amount of time.

2. Business acumen. Notice the way the potential partner(s) do business and consider whether or not it aligns with your standards of ethics and integrity. Observe the character, communication skills, and personality of the senior leaders.

3. Accounting records. Investigate for fraud, tax evasion, embezzlement, mishandling or misappropriation of funds.

4. Credit checks. Depending on the form of partnership being considered, one party's negative credit may impact all parties; even after the partnership has dissolved.

5. Background checks. Look for criminal activity or involvements that do not align with your vision, mission, purpose, or those of your key investors and supporters.

6. Key personnel. Consider who you will inherit as business associates, as well as who you are willing to terminate or replace from your own team during onboarding.

Empowering Scripture

"Two are better than one, because they have a good return for their labor: If either of them falls down, one can help the other up. But pity anyone who falls and has no one to help them up."

Ecclesiastes 4:9-10

Write now! Don't forget the ideas you have while reading this section:_____

_____

_____

_____

_____

_____

_____

_____

_____

_____

_____

_____

_____

_____

_____

_____

_____

_____

_____

_____

_____

LAUNCH

Start with Confidence

Arriving to this point means two things: (1) you are genuinely sincere about learning all you can to have the best business launch possible, and (2) you are likely on information overload. Take a moment to recap all that you've read. Look over the notes you made after each section. If you didn't think so before, you should definitely know now that you are a businessperson! It is time to begin stacking your building blocks. Be confident and allow the following checklist to guide you:

- ❏ **BLOCK 1: Build a Foundation.** Seek God for guidance and and know why you're stepping into entrepreneurship.

- ❏ **BLOCK 2: Understand the Problem.** Decide "what" and "who's" problem you are going to solve.

- ❏ **BLOCK 3: Start Dreaming.** Brainstorm on what your business will be. Write the vision and register it.

- ❏ **BLOCK 4: Invent Products & Services.** Decide on what you'll offer, and create the branding for it

- ❏ **BLOCK 5: Network.** Join networking circles and attend events that will generate brand recognition.

- ❏ **BLOCK 6: Experience & Competence.** Make a list of all of your experience, education and special training.

- ❏ **BLOCK 7: Specify the Market.** Know your niche. Understand your target market and create your ideal customer.

- ❑ **BLOCK 8: Summarize the competition.** Find out who is solving problems for your target market and what's being offered.
- ❑ **BLOCK 9: Promoting & Marketing.** Create a website, set up social media accounts, take photos and set up interviews.
- ❑ **BLOCK 10: Ethics & Integrity.** Think strategically about delivering quality products and experiences.
- ❑ **BLOCK 11: Risks & Rewards.** Responsibly determine what you can invest and have a plan for challenges and setbacks.
- ❑ **BLOCK 12: Shipping & Fulfillment.** Find an efficient and cost effective way to get products or services to the customer.
- ❑ **BLOCK 13: Objectives & Goals.** Have a strategic plan, KPIs and action items that help you stay focused on growth.
- ❑ **BLOCK 14: Negotiate Partnerships.** Consider the benefits of working with others as partners or as a referral network.

Once you have executed the items on this checklist, you are ready to host a launch party and let others know all about your business and your brand. Note: If you desire to outsource these items, finding a professional whose work you "trust" will be Important.

Congratulations on starting your entrepreneurial journey!

KEY TERMS

Speaking Entrepre-nese!

Every field has its own lingo. Such is the case with entrepreneurship. One of the first tasks for anyone new to the startup space is to learn "entrepre-nese!" That's right! There are some terms and phrases that come with the territory, and to avoid intimidation, being familiar with the following words, acronyms, and abbreviations is helpful. Note: There are other concepts and words that are introduced in greater detail throughout the book. However, these listed here may not be engaged as fully.

A

Affiliate Marketing – Earning commission by promoting products or services of other individuals or companies that lead to sales. This includes the arrangement of using others to promote ones' own products or services by offering commission.

AIDA – Attention, Interest, Desire, Action. This acronym describes the steps of a customer's buying process. Marketers aim to lead their consumers through each of these stages in order to gain a conversion.

Angel Investor – One who invests their own capital into new businesses for monetary equity in the business.

B

B2B – Business to Business. B2B companies market their products or services to other businesses.

B2C – Business to Consumer. B2C companies market their products or services directly to consumers.

Barter – The exchange of products or services directly between individuals, groups, or businesses likely excluding monetary currency.

Business Plan – A document or presentation that overviews purpose, strategies, outcomes, the target market, risk assessments, and projections for a business. This is usually required from capital investors and funding sources.

C

Cash Flow – Cash flowing in and out of a business. The goal is a positive cash flow, when there is more money coming in than going out. The opposite is a negative cash flow.

CLV – Customer Lifetime Value. CLV is a prediction of the total net profit a customer will be worth throughout the entire duration of their business with you.

Conversion Rate – A conversion refers to whatever action you desire from your customers (e.g., a purchase, subscription, etc.) The conversion rate is calculated by dividing the total number of conversions by the number of visitors to your website.

Copyright – A declaration of ownership or legal rights to a specific arrangement of words, scientific work, or art.

CPA – Cost per Action. CPA is an online advertising payment model where payment is based solely on qualifying actions such as sales or registrations; Also note the separate but more common reference of CPA to a *Certified Public Accountant.*

CPC – Cost per Click. A website using a CPC payment program will charge customers based on the number of times users click on their ad or link. This is often based on a daily budget, meaning the ad is pulled from the rotation as soon as the budget is reached each day.

CRM – Customer Relationship Management. A CRM system uses technology to organize and automate customer interactions.

This enables a company to create more meaningful and strategic communication based on demographic data, buying history and industry information.

CTA – Call to Action. Providing direction to your audience prompting them to take a specific action (e.g., call today, visit us online, etc.)

CTR – Click-Through Rate. CTR is a metric used to determine the success of an online ad. It is expressed as a percentage which is calculated by dividing the number of clicks by total impressions and multiplying by one hundred. A high percentage indicates an effective ad.

D

Due Diligence – Taking the necessary steps to properly research a business before making an investment or entering into any form of partnership.

E

E-commerce – E-commerce is an abbreviation of *electronic commerce* and refers to any type of business that involves the transfer of information online. E-commerce marketing strategies aim to drive users to a website to purchase a product or service.

Equity ownership – Having ownership in a company based on the stock acquired in that company.

F

Franchise – A business with multiple locations that can be purchased individually.

Fringe Benefits – Employer provided benefits to employees that are in addition to a base salary.

G

General Partnership – An organization structured with general partners that share in specifically outlined aspects of the business, such as administration, profits, loses, and personal liability.

H

Hard Launch – The grand opening of a business or the official release of a product or service.

Home Based Business – A business with the owner's home address as the primary business office.

HTML – Hypertext Markup Language. HTML is a coding language used to make hypertext documents for use on the Internet. A block of text is surrounded by codes that indicate how it should appear in the browser.

I

Inbound Marketing – This type of marketing refers to strategies that bring consumers in, rather than marketers having to go out to reach consumers. Inbound marketing earns the attention of the audience using tactics such as search engine optimization, social networks, pay-per-click advertising or blogging.

Intellectual Property – Thoughts, concepts, lyrics, plans, phrases, or ideas created from one's own mind and usually protected by copyright, patent, or trademark laws.

Intrapreneur – A person who operates entrepreneurially within a larger company or corporate environment.

J

Joint Venture – Two or more businesses entering into a business partnership and sharing profits and losses.

K

K-commerce – The exchange of knowledge capital in knowledge-based economies in which knowledge is considered a very real form of currency.

KPI – Key Performance Indicator. A KPI is a metric used to evaluate the success of an organization or campaign. This is a way to quantify a company's goals in order to ensure business objectives are being met.

L

Limited Partnership – A business in which one or more partners control daily operations, that is also funded by limited (or silent) partners who are is liable for losses based on their capital investment.

Line of Credit – A loan in which the borrower makes regular payments and pays interest only on the amount of funds actually used.

LLC – Limited Liability Company. A business that is not taxable and in which the owners are not held personally responsible for the debt of the company.

M

Margins – Percentages of net sales revenue. It is the difference between the seller's cost of production and manufacturing per unit and the selling price of the final product or service.

Marketing – Practices of communicating a core concept of a product or service to a target market that includes promoting, advertising, pricing, packaging, and selling strategies.

MoM – Month-Over-Month. MOM is a form of comparing a metric based on the previous month, usually expressed in a percentage. Similarly, data can be compared quarter-over-quarter (QoQ) or year-over-year (YoY.)

N

Network Marketing – A business that utilizes a distributor network to promote and sell the products or services of the business.

Networking – Connecting with individuals or businesses to establish acquaintances or to form business relationships

Net Worth – The monetary sum of all of a business's assets. This includes the value of capital and property as well as liabilities.

Niche – A niche is a smaller section of the larger global market created through a process of narrowing data called *data segmentation*.

O

Outsourcing – Contracting another businesses to provide operational services.

P

Partnership – Two or more persons coming together as partners in a business, and each filing taxes to reflect equal shares of profit and loss.

Patent – Legal rights to a creation or invention that prevents others from duplicating it or profiting from it for a limited time.

Q

Q Ratio – A calculation of dividing the market value of capital assets by the cost to replace them. An example of where this calculation is useful would be if a q ratio was low, prompting a business to purchase used replacements instead of new ones.

Quality by Design – Building quality into a good or service from its inception to its final tangible product.

R

Revenue – Money earned from the sale of a product or service.

ROI – Return on Investment. ROI is a performance measurement that considers profits in relation to the capital invested. For example: if your company spent $10,000 on an advertising campaign and made a total of $15,000 as a result, your ROI would be 50 percent.

S

SEM – Search Engine Marketing. SEM is a type of Internet marketing that aims to improve a website's visibility in search engine results via optimization and advertising.

SEO – Search Engine Optimization. SEO is the process of developing a technical plan to ensure effective use of search engines as a marketing tool. Some common SEO tactics include targeting strategic keywords, building quality links to your website and encouraging social sharing.

SERP – Search Engine Results Page. SERPs are the list of webpages presented to you after entering a query into a search engine such as Google. The higher your website appears in the SERPs, the more likely a user is to click on it.

Soft Launch – When a new business is launched to a limited or private audience before the general public.

Sole Proprietorship – A business owned by an individual and taxed as a personal account.

T

Target Market – A specific audience that advertisements and marketing efforts are directed to. This could be based on relevance, prior interest, or any demographical information.

Trademark – Legal rights to words, names, symbols, tunes, or color patterns that distinguish a specific product or service. Trademarks can be renewed forever as long as they are in use.

U

Uber-wealthy – A phrase based on the German prefix "Uber," which means "super" or "excess" referencing the elite wealthy upper class.

USP – Unique Selling Proposition. USP refers to the features or characteristics that differentiate a product or service from competitors.

V

Value Proposition – A document communicating the value of a product or service and an explanation of why one should purchase or invest in it.

VC – Venture Capitalist. A person who provides capital in exchange for equity in a business.

W

Wage – Monetary compensation based on an hourly, daily, weekly, monthly, or annual rate.

WOMM – Word of Mouth Marketing. This type of marketing is when a company actively encourages an audience to share a message with others. This can be done by seeding information within particular networks, rewarding loyal members or leveraging social media.

X

X-Mark Signature – It is a mark allowed to be made by a person in lieu of their own signature if they are unable to render a full signature at the time. Making the "X" mark reflects that the person has reviewed the document and approves of its contents. This marking must be witnessed to be legally valid.

Y

Yield – Income earned from an investment annually calculated as a percentage.

Z

ZBB – Zero Based Budgeting. Cash-flow budgets that start from zero every year, with no pre-authorized funding and assumes no present commitment exists.

Zipper Clause – A clause that expresses that the document contains the complete agreement negotiated by all parties. Any added stipulations must be added to the original agreement in writing and be signed by all parties.

About the Author

Dr. Iria Loraine Abram, founder of EPHRIAM HOUSE, Inc. (EH), is originally from South Central Los Angeles, CA. She had a gift for consulting and incorporated EH in 2005. In 2007 she was appointed to be the Director of Marketing for a major property development and management corporation and from this she acquired much experience and knowledge, eventually building an intricate network of executives and businesses that allow her to function as a business broker for marketing and branding projects. She has earned a Bachelor of Arts degree in Leadership and Administration, a Master of Arts degree in Christian Education, and most recently a Doctorate of Ministry degree. She is also a certified Leadership Coach and is currently serving Beulah Heights University as the Doctor of Ministry Program Director. Notably, Dr. Abram founded *Yield! Youth Leadership Development* in 2011, and a global academic organization, *Sigma Gamma Theta – The Society of Women in Theology*, in the spring of 2018. As a wife and mother of two sons, her personal mission is to be a bridge between the faith community and the startup ecosystem; restoring value to kingdom minded Christian visionaries to help them pursue and build their God given dreams and passions.

subscribe: ephriamhouse.com
email: help@ephriamhouse.com
mailing: PO Box 92328 Atlanta, GA 30314
contact: (404) 623-5906
social: @ephriamhouse

Made in the USA
Coppell, TX
10 November 2023

24075061R10089